CHURCHES IN WALES
and their treasures

By the same author:

Eglwysi Cymru a'u Trysorau

Y Teithwyr yng Nghymru, 1750–1850

John Parker's Tour through Wales and its Churches

Churches in Wales
and their treasures

Edgar W. Parry

First published in 2011

© Edgar W. Parry/Llygad Gwalch 2011

ISBN: 978-1-84524-178-0

Cover design: Lynwen Jones

Published by
Llygad Gwalch, Ysgubor Plas, Llwyndyrys,
Pwllheli, Gwynedd, Wales, LL53 6NG.
Tel: 01758 750432
e-mail: books@carreg-gwalch.com
www.carreg-gwalch.com

Dedication

I gofio am fy merch Annwen

In memory of my daughter Annwen

Acknowledgements

*I have pleasure in offering my thanks to those
who were so willing to ensure that the churches
I visited were open to me, and who gave me so much
help during my research. Thanks too for their
readiness to answer my numerous questions.*

*I am thankful for happy co-operation
with Gwasg Carreg Gwalch, as usual,
and for their acceptance and publication of this book.*

*My grateful thanks are also due to the editor,
Jen Llywelyn, for her helpful suggestions,
understanding and support.*

Any errors which may remain are mine entirely.

Contents

Preface

In most of the towns and parishes of Wales, the parish church still remains the most interesting and ancient building. Each church is unique and each one is worthy of a visit, as they all contain some objects of beauty which are not to be found anywhere else, and are treasures in their own right. There is some indefinable serenity and peacefulness to be found within their walls, and they are always there whatever may happen to us.

The church has played an essential part in every community from the beginning of time and it has been the heart of the community which grew up around it. As well as a place of worship, this is where parish business was transacted, and the local market and sports were held either within its walls or in its churchyard. Churches, more than anything else, remind us of our past. On any count, spiritual or artistic, they are assets beyond price.

Unfortunately, the number of worshippers is dwindling, but it appears that an increasing number of people are anxious to visit churches to study their history and appreciate the treasures which are often to be found in them. A careful study of any parish church will provide an illustration of the framework of life in the community, as it has undoubtedly been linked with the lives of our ancestors for centuries. The church has always had something to offer every generation, whatever problems they have to face.

It is true that the architecture of parish churches in rural Wales cannot be compared to the architecture of the many magnificent castles we have, but each one, nevertheless, is important and interesting. In some of our remote churches you will find some incomparable medieval treasure. Where else, indeed, can you find such wealth? Where else can you find better examples of medieval carving? All these treasures are worthy of our attention and our support for their safe keeping. They are a priceless national heritage and cannot be studied anywhere else.

In Wales we have lost a large number of screens from our churches over the years through the instructions of kings and the orders of bishops, especially following the Reformation, and also through lack of care and attention. Many churches were lost during the Victorian era, when they were left to deteriorate, or the work of their restoration was given to architects and builders who were quite ignorant of the work that needed to be done. This was the period when many medieval screens were removed, and either sold as firewood to the parishioners or to enrich the homes of wealthy landowners. Little or no consideration was given to the intricate work they contained, or to their historical importance. Many of the churches were rebuilt or repaired without the feeling of sacredness which belonged to those who established these early churches. Could it be that because we have lost that ideal we are only now beginning to realise our mistakes?

But what of the future? Are we going to allow our ancient churches to fall into disrepair once again? A few years ago, the then Archbishop of Canterbury said that the Church of England was experiencing serious financial difficulties and warned that it could not be expected to maintain all its churches because 'we have inherited so many buildings which do not reflect modern liturgical practices'. The fact that so many of our churches have had to close their doors because of lack of support certainly poses some grave problems, not least of which is to decide what is to become of their treasures. I feel strongly that the medieval screens, for example, are indeed national treasures, and sooner or later we will have to accept responsibility for them. How can a congregation of, say, forty or less be expected to shoulder the financial responsibility for the upkeep of these treasures? Their fabrics are all ancient and in many cases are in less satisfactory repair than one would wish, and repairs are becoming ever more costly.

My intention in this book is to draw attention to some of these treasures which are unique in themselves, in the hope that it will awaken our awareness of them and make us willing to do all that is possible, within our ability, to secure their future. A great responsibility is placed upon us, and I hope that we can measure up to that responsibility.

But before we can appreciate these particular treasures properly it is important that we have some knowledge of the history of the Church through the centuries so as to understand the reasoning behind some of the things which we are likely to encounter when we visit the parish church. For example, if we are to appreciate the beauty which is to be found in the screens, then we need to understand their importance to the traditions of the Church in its early years.

I am not making any reference to the stained glass windows which are to be found, although it is impossible not to mention in passing the outstanding Jesse window at St Dyfnog's church in Llanrhaeadr-yng-Nghinmeirch, Denbighshire. Neither am I referring to the sixteenth-century Flemish glass at St Gwenllwyfo's church, Llanwenllwyfo, Anglesey – you will need to visit the Metropolitan Museum in New York to see anything comparable. The reason for this decision is that there are already standard works on such windows. Likewise, I am not dealing with the Welsh cathedrals because here again numerous books are already available.

My aim in this book is to try and answer some of the questions which are likely to be asked by the layman when visiting any church, thus making such visits more enjoyable, and to have a better appreciation of the treasures which they contain.

It is impossible in a book such as this to discuss every church. Therefore, I have included my personal selection only, acknowledging at the same time that a great number of churches worthy of inclusion have had to be omitted. I hope, however, that the book will generate a renewed interest in the ancient churches which are to be found in the Welsh countryside – and even in these remote areas, they all share the charms and merits of much larger churches. I believe that the churches which I have selected contain a fair representation of the best screens to be found in Wales.

Edgar W. Parry
Caernarfon
March 2011

Chapter 1

The early years

Each period in history has left its mark upon subsequent periods, and we have a responsibility to look at those periods and learn from them. However, it is not the bare bones of history that are important, but rather what we learn from them, and by so doing we will quickly realise how one period appears to merge into another.

Wales is rich in its castles, and for a long time it was thought that it had nothing else to offer in the field of ancient architecture. However, what about ancient churches? When they are given only a cursory inspection, there is a danger that their more interesting features are overlooked. With the fragmentation of the country into small parishes, a seemingly insignificant parish church can easily be ignored. This must not mean that the churches are unworthy of attention, as each one is unique and an asset beyond price. It is easy to travel through centuries of history when a visit is made to our churches.

In the process of learning from the past, the parish church is very important. From the beginning of time, mankind has resorted to one form of worship or another, be it earth, sun, moon, fire or water, or indeed anything which was capable of supplying his daily needs.

When looking at the ancient churches of Wales today we can experience various chapters in the history of our parishes. The church provided unity and stability within the parishes. It is still the heart of the community and that heart has been beating from time immemorial.

Our cathedrals, and likewise our churches, were the culmination of architectural achievements of their day. They demonstrate an enormous commitment in time, skill and expenditure, and their erection was undertaken by the best craftsmen of the time. They each represent centuries of history and culture of the parish, and even the most insignificant church can be as interesting and captivating as any cathedral.

However, not only architectural achievement and grandeur can be found in the parish church, but rather centuries of the history of Christianity. Each generation has used the church in a different fashion in accordance with their understanding of the Christian faith, and all this can be discovered from the fabric of the church. They have all been designed for a particular form of service. In the Orthodox Church, the priest was separated from the congregation by a solid screen or iconostasis, whilst at the Quakers' meeting houses the seats face each other and there is no priest. As the form of service changed over the years there would also be a need for some structural changes within churches.

The parish church fulfilled the spiritual and the social needs of the community. It was involved with all human feelings and emotions whether they were happy or distressing, and in addition, it gave pleasure during feast days, which were very important in the church calendar.

Inside many churches ancient oak chests are to be found, sometimes hewn from solid tree trunks. They were fitted with three locks: the priest would have one key, and the other two would have been held by the churchwardens, and all three would have to be present when the chest was opened. In them were kept not only the valuable church plate and vestments, but also all the parish records and accounts. The presence of these chests reminds us that the church was the centre not only of the religious life, but also the public life, of the community.

Public notices are still to be found in the church porch, and this reminds us of the days when much of the parish business was carried out in the church itself. This is where the children were baptised and where marriages were solemnized, and it was in the churchyard that they were buried. Those who had broken their vows had to walk around the church dressed in a white sheet as a penance. Francis Kilvert noted in his diary that at Clyro several of his parishioners 'used to go to the church door at midnight on Midsummer's Eve to hear the names of those who were to die within the year'.

The interior walls would have been lime-washed and some would have paintings on them. Apart from their decorative effect, they would have illustrated the Christian story to a largely illiterate congregation. Incidents from the life of Christ and of the early saints would have filled some of the walls. Over the chancel arch would have been found a painting of the Day of Judgement, or 'The Doom', as it was called. This would have shown open graves at the bottom. On one side would be 'the Good' ascending to heaven to be received by Christ, and on the other side 'the Bad' would be seen descending to hell to be tortured by devils. The iconoclasts of Edward VI or Cromwell obliterated these wonderful paintings with limewash, but it is surprising how many are being re-discovered after centuries of limewashing. These early churches would have been quite unlike the hovels in which the population would have lived.

If we are to understand all that can be learnt by a careful

study of our ancient churches then we must look to their origin to see how and why the Celtic church was different from those to be found in Europe. We must follow the changes in the form of services and customs as they developed over the centuries.

It is reasonable to assume that the druids would have continued as priests of the new religion on their conversion to Christianity, and they would have used their pagan sites within their stone circles for their services. A letter from Pope Gregory in the seventh century stated:

> I have come to the conclusion that the temples of the idols in England should not on any account be destroyed. Augustine must smash the idols, but the temples themselves should be sprinkled with holy water and altars set upon them, in which the relics are to be enclosed. For we are to take advantage of the well-built temples by purifying them from the devil-worship and dedicating them to the true God.

Many of today's churchyards follow the same circular pagan circles and would explain why so many circular churchyards are to be found in Wales. On close inspection of some of them, the standing stones are to be found incorporated in the churchyard wall. In many churches can be seen images of the 'Green Man' either painted or carved on the screens. This is a human face with foliage protruding from its mouth and ears, and it originally represented the spirit of the forest and provider of a plentiful harvest. The term is derived from the Anglo-Saxon word meaning 'to germinate' or 'to become green'. When early Christians moved into the area they chose a site already made use of in much earlier times, and the circular churchyard provides the link between the two periods.

At Ysbyty Cynfyn, between Pumlumon and Devil's Bridge (*Pontarfynach*), five of the remaining standing stones have been incorporated into the churchyard wall whilst others have been used as gateposts. Ysbyty Cynfyn was on the trail to the Cistercian abbey of Strata Florida, and in the twelfth century offered much needed assistance and shelter to the early pilgrims.

Entrance to the churchyard is often through a lych gate, that is, a gate with a roof over it. Prior to interment this is where the coffin would rest and be protected to some extent from the weather while awaiting the arrival of the priest. It is called a lych gate from the Old English term 'lic', meaning corpse, and in some areas it is called a 'corpse gate'.

Early parish registers will contain references to 'Burial in Wool'. In 1667 and 1678 Burial in Wool Acts were passed that were intended to promote the wool trade. They required that corpses should be buried in wool (except those who died of the plague). The officiating priest was required to certify that the deceased had been buried in wool. Failure to comply resulted in a fine of £5 being levied on both the estate of the deceased and on those associated with the burial

The churchyard also ensured security during civil disorder, and animals were herded in, in the knowledge that they would be safe. For a long time the area to the north of the church would have been used as the village playground for wrestling, football, tennis and even cockfighting.

Before Christianity, burial places had long been used, according to Sir Mortimer Wheeler, 'for communal and secular no less than religious purposes in an age when the two were essentially one and indivisible'. Consequently, many churchyards are of greater antiquity than the churches associated with them. Whilst the early Christians completely rejected paganism, they were nevertheless quite prepared to continue with the use of the old pagan burial sites.

In Wales in the sixth century an open place or enclosure (*llan*) was set aside for religious purposes and for burials and it was much later that the term became to mean 'church'.

At one time, it was a popular belief that the churchyards were circular so that the devil could not find a corner to hide.

The term 'Celtic church' is perhaps misleading and whilst it had its own distinctive features, it was nevertheless much later to become part of the Catholic church, but a church in which there was little uniformity. One major disagreement concerned the date for Easter, which in the Celtic church was calculated by means of the old system devised in 314, unlike that of Rome which had been adopted in 457. Wales retained the old system until 768. With regard to the termination of the Easter controversy Professor J. E. Lloyd wrote: 'The Welsh Church still retained in many respects the marks of the monastic and Celtic origin, and there was still room left in Wales for the growth of distinctive features of Church life'.

A popular perceived characteristic of the Celt was that of the hermit in his isolated and remote cell. The hermit preferred isolation and his cell was to be found in many offshore islands such as Bardsey (*Enlli*) or Caldey (*Ynys Bŷr*), or in remote mountainous locations like Pennant Melangell. It was at sites such as these that he would have felt safe from the troubled times he lived in. By the end of the sixth century he felt that it was imperative for him to find these remote sites because of the plague of 549. This became the 'Age of the Saints', when Christianity really gained ground in Wales. As time went by these remote sites became sacred and attracted local people to worship there, and some were later developed into parish churches.

As the population increased and settled in the lower plains the churches were also re-located. It is only the names of most of the ancient sites that are known today, whilst others were developed to become important abbeys, such as Bardsey, off the Llŷn peninsula – one of the most ancient of all sanctuaries of the Celtic church. Dubricus is said to have settled and died there probably before AD 540, and even at that early date Bardsey was evidently a well-known sanctuary. Although the early churches were very primitive in design, they did have a considerable influence upon the style of church buildings for many centuries.

Sir Gilbert Scott maintained that the basic construction of the Celtic church followed the design of the room in Jerusalem where the disciples used to meet, and that construction strengthened the eastern influence upon our churches. Consequently, the design of the early churches was very simple. The Mass was celebrated at the eastern end of the church behind the screen. The rood was later added, with the carving of the crucified Christ with the Virgin Mary and St John on either side. The church would not have a steeple and a handbell would be used. Giraldus Cambrensis reports, 'In the church at Glascwm in Elfael there is a handbell which has almost miraculous powers. It is reported to have belonged to St David and it is called a 'Bangu'. These early bells are extremely rare, but Gwyddelen's Bell has been safely returned to the church at

Dolwyddelan, having been in the possession of the Gwydir family for generations, and it is important that it should have been returned to its traditional home. It is unlikely, however, that this bell could be earlier than the tenth century, and its design is typical of other bells of that period.

Bells were introduced into the Celtic church in the sixth century and came into general use in the eighth century. In the medieval period, the bells of parish churches marked the canonical hours and summoned the faithful to worship. They tolled the curfew and the angelus, warned of invasion and alarm, and announced the death of parishioners. They celebrated baptism, weddings and feast days. At the Reformation, many church bells were either silenced or removed and it was only during the Elizabethan period that they were restored. Inscriptions on Tudor and post-Reformation bells tend to be secular in character and often incorporate the name of the bell-founder and of the benefactor.

As there were no fonts in the early churches it was the custom for baptism to be performed in a well near the church. It is surprising to find today how many are still associated with the churches. Over the centuries, folklore has been woven around these wells; many were said to have miraculous powers and referred to as 'the saint's well'. These wells were recognized as sacred before Christianity. The practice of using water from associated wells is still used to this day for baptism in a number of churches.

It is unreasonable to compare the churches of Wales with those in England for a variety of reasons. In the mountainous regions of Wales, the population was very sparse, the native stone was difficult to work with, and while Gothic architecture was developing in England Wales was embroiled with difficulties. Sir John Wynn of Gwydir, in his book *The History of the Gwydir Family*, gives a very vivid description of life in Caernarfonshire and throughout north Wales in the fifteenth century. When Meredydd ap Ieuan was leaving Crug near Caernarfon he wrote:

> he was minded to have returned to his inheritance in Evioneth where there was nothing but killinge and fighting, where upon he did purchase a lease of the castle and Frithes of dolthelan. And in Ysbyty Ifan he found a large thinge, w'ch had privilege of sanctuarie a peculiar iurisdiction not governed by the king's laws, a receptacle of thieves and murtherers, whoe safely beinge warranted there by lawe and safe from incursions and roberrie . . . and that he had rather fight with outlawes and thieves than with his own blood and kindred, for if I live in myne owne house in Evioneth I must eyther kill myne owne kinsmen or be killed by them.

In view of circumstances such as these, it is not difficult to understand why the early churches of Wales merely fulfilled the immediate needs of the people and were without any outstanding architectural features.

The best examples to be found in Wales belong to the Tudor period, when the relationship between Wales and England achieved some semblance of normality. This was the period that saw the reconstruction of the churches at Clynnog, Bangor and Beaumaris in the north, and Carmarthen and Tenby in the south.

The Celtic church had its special features:

(i) the square east end with a small window as opposed to the apse;

(ii) the altar was behind a screen instead of being brought forward under a canopy;

(iii) a south door instead of the western portal.

In addition, these special features were quite different from any other country in western Europe.

In the east, the apse had been adopted for an architectural reason rather than from any liturgical reason, but with regard to our chancel screens, Sir Gilbert Scott maintains that:

> We seem to see an eastern influence, the same in fact which led to the solid screen, or iconostasis which in the Greek church completely conceals the whole rite from the view of the faithful. To the same origin we must refer the feeling which prevailed in England all through the Middle Ages, and which led to the erection of those high chancel screens surmounted by imagery and paintings, by which the chancel arch was often filled up. The tendency which is shown in all this, and which is quite characteristic of English Medievalism is so entirely opposite to that of the basilica, is the expression that it is impossible to suppose that one is derived from the other. We cannot avoid the conclusion that the two represent two separate and independent traditions, whose distinction is coeval with the very foundation of the Christian church.

The altar in these churches would have been covered with a white cloth, on which would have been placed the relics of the saint, such as a bell, book and staff, in exactly the same way as Geraldus Cambrensis refers to them. There would have been very little light in the building, with just the small window in the chancel and an open door providing the only other light. This was the state of affairs at Llanfaglan church near Caernarfon until the transept was built in the early 1600s. As the priest was the only one who possessed a book there was little need for any additional illumination for the congregation. The floor was of bare earth and the walls would have been limewashed. This was the situation in many churches until the early years of the nineteenth century. Many of the early travellers to Wales refer to the churches in this manner, and to the practice of burials within the church. An examination of any parish register will reveal entries showing the purchase of straw for covering the floor for important occasions in the church calendar, such as Easter.

Very little change took place until the end of the thirteenth and the beginning of the fourteenth centuries, when the Latin or Gregorian liturgy replaced the British one. This was also the period when chancels were added to a number of churches such as at Llangelynnin and Gyffin, and the ancient Welsh bard Cynddelw (fl. 1155–1200) refers in one of his poems to Llanllugan in Montgomeryshire with its special place for the Mass.

After the insurrection of Owain Glyndŵr Wales became more stable, and the reign of the Tudors from 1485 saw a general improvement in the country in general, together with a gradual increase in population. By the fifteenth century and after the Reformation, more substantial churches were built and bell towers were erected.

Churches have always been designed for a particular form of service; any change in their design is reflected by change in the form of service and can be followed from one generation to the next. The services from the Common Prayer Book and the long sermons were to be audible to the whole congregation and therefore the churches of the seventeenth and eighteenth centuries were either rebuilt or adapted for that purpose. Sir Christopher Wren said: 'It is enough if they (the Romanists) hear the murmur of the Mass and see the Elevation of the Host, but ours are fitted as auditories'. Consequently, the nave was filled with high box pews that also gave some measure of protection from the cold.

As the sermon had now become the rival of the sacraments, the pulpit was the most conspicuous piece of furniture. Nothing was too much for its adornment and an imposing sounding board or tester surmounted it, sometimes as high as the church itself. The square box pews governed the height of the pulpit, and a prominent pulpit ensured the congregation could both see and hear the priest. Sometimes a 'three-decker' pulpit could be found ascending vertically with separate areas for the use of the clerk, the reader and the preacher.

If these early churches lacked architectural merit it does not mean that they are of no interest, or that they lack character. The repairs carried out in the nineteenth century may have destroyed many of their original features but these old buildings still required as much understanding and sympathy when they were repaired as they did when they were originally built.

Chapter 2

Abbeys and monasteries

In the early years of Christianity, the establishment of the monastic ideal became very popular in Wales. Many monastic establishments were set up. They became famous for their self-sacrifice, and were established in remote areas and off-shore islands where the monastic tradition of escaping from secular life could be maintained. The ideal of seclusion was of the utmost importance.

The thirteenth century was the golden age of monasticism in its second phase after the early years of the Celtic church. It was the natural progression from the life of the anchorite of that period.

The Cistercians were the most important order in Wales and they were responsible for the magnificent abbeys such as Strata Florida, Cymer, Cwm Hir, Valle Crucis and Tintern. The main purpose of these grand abbeys was for prayer, to offer hospitality and to dispense charity. The ancient Welsh bards offer ample testimony to the generosity of their abbots.

Some of their abbeys became very rich and were the owners of vast tracts of land. They also received substantial income in tithes from their churches. Their estates were managed so efficiently that they became victims of their own success. As their administrative responsibilities increased, they were obliged to increase their establishments with *conversi* and paid officials. The *conversi* were laymen who had 'turned' to the service of God, and were generally occupied in manual work and included skilled craftsmen such as stonemasons. But from the mid fourteenth century the *conversi* began deserting the monasteries in large numbers, attracted by improved wages and working conditions. As their importance and influence decreased the abbeys were forced to lease their lands to their friends and tenants. They were certainly a tempting target for Henry VIII for dissolution and seizure of their wealth for his own purposes. He was also to transfer their lands to private impropriators for various favours instead of restoring them to their rightful owners – the Welsh parochial clergy. The Church and the poor were robbed of their inheritance.

The Cistercians were not the only order to establish themselves in Wales. The Benedictines (the 'black monks') and the Augustinians selected ancient monastic sites for their houses, and where there were survivors of an earlier community they joined it, such as on Bardsey island off the coast of Caernarfonshire. The Franciscan and Dominican friars, whose popularity in the thirteenth century was in part attributable to their preference of going out into the world to preach rather than withdrawing into a monastic building, also established their houses here, as did the Premonstratensians.

The advent of monasticism to Wales was to some extent associated with the Norman barons, and in south Wales there was a close association between the abbeys and the Norman castles. The abbeys were sometimes used as strongholds for the Normans. In time, both the military and religious establishments came to be reviled because they had become houses for French and English monks at the exclusion of the Welsh. In north Wales, where the Norman power was not so strong, the abbeys were subject to different influences.

Cistercian abbeys were built in secluded valleys so that the monks could work their land and tend to their sheep without any outside influences or danger. They were farmers and shepherds, and this made them very popular with the Welsh. Their life of austere simplicity, in conjunction with hard work, made it easy for the Welsh people to recognise the revival of the primitive simplicity associated with their own native saints. A Cistercian abbey was a well organised self-supporting community. The monks were successful farmers and employers of labour. By the thirteenth century they had improved their lands and become very successful breeders of sheep and cattle, and carried on an extensive trade in wool.

Ambitious though monastic life might have been, it did not always fulfil its ambitions. When Giraldus Cambrensis accompanied Archbishop Baldwin on his tour through Wales when the latter was recruiting men for the Crusades, he made numerous references to the abbeys; sometimes his remarks were favourable and at other times he was most critical. On one occasion he felt that corruption seemed to be the rule of the day, and with particular reference to the Cistercians he said:

> The Cistercian Order which derived from the Benedictines clung tenaciously to its original vow of poverty and holiness, and, in the beginning, it too was much praised and commended, but there again, ambition, the blind mother of all our ills, took possession of it . . . I am inclined to think that the lust for possessions, so noisily acclaimed the whole world over, springs in this case from good intentions. The monks of the Cistercian Order, are in fact extremely abstemious, busy themselves unceasingly to provide hospitality for all

and sundry, offering limitless charity to pilgrims and the needy. They do not live as others do on fixed incomes but on the sweat of their brows, and their own good management. That is why they are so anxious to acquire land from the proceeds of which they can meet the demands of hospitality. They are constantly on the look out for rich lands and broad pastures.

Gerald was firmly of the opinion that the damnable stigma of ambition should be removed from their holy order.

The roots of the Cistercian order are to be found in Citeaux in France. After a shaky start it became a great force in Europe by 1115, with their influence and their monasteries increasing. By 1131 they had established their abbey in Tintern (*Tyndyrn*) on the banks of the river Wye and in 1140 they established another at Whitland (*Hendy-gwyn*). The Cistercians became a thoroughly Welsh order by adoption and they associated themselves with the national interest of the people. By the time of Owain Glyndŵr's uprising (1400–1412) their abbeys had become dilapidated. Whilst the Priory in Cardiff had been saved, the great abbey at Cwm Hir never recovered. By 1412 Margam had been destroyed; the abbot and monks were turned out and became beggars. The uprising brought with it a decline in monastic life.

The situation at Strata Florida was very similar to that of all other abbeys, and by the beginning of the sixteenth century the number of monks there had been considerably reduced.

By 1525-26 Henry VIII wanted a divorce from his wife Catherine of Aragon but this was refused by Pope Clement VII. By 1532 Henry was more determined than ever to be rid of his wife because his mistress, Anne Boleyn, was pregnant: in order to secure the succession he did not want the child to be born illegitimate – particularly if she should be delivered of a boy. In 1533 Henry secretly married Anne Boleyn and in the same year she bore him a daughter – Elizabeth. Archbishop Cranmer later announced that his marriage to Catherine had been invalid.

The covetousness and laxity of the clergy during the fifteenth century had done much to undermine their prestige in the public eye, and the effectiveness of the monasteries had been a persistent scandal for a hundred years or more. However, it was the personal quarrel of Henry VIII with the Pope that brought to a head the public dissatisfaction with a corrupt papacy and its agents. Reform, therefore, was occasioned by papal procrastination concerning the 'King's Great Matter' – the dissolution of Henry's marriage to Catherine of Aragon.

The movement towards reform was consequently so spontaneous and vigorous that it was understandably accepted. The easy-going tolerance of many people to the religious changes of the sixteenth century led many to accept the Reformation without scruples. Another factor was the greed of the king and his officials who roamed the country at the time feeding on the spoils of the prostrate Church.

Despite the break with Rome, Henry VIII consistently opposed the Reforming movement and remained a convinced traditionalist in matters of doctrine and church government, and it was not until after his death in 1547 that doctrinal Protestantism became official policy.

In 1534 the Act of Supremacy was passed and Henry broke with Rome and was acknowledged as Supreme Head of the Church of England under Christ.

Once Henry had been acknowledged as Head of the Church it was but a small step for him to turn his attention towards the abbeys and their assets. It was estimated at the time that in Wales they contributed £3000 a year – a pretty substantial amount. They had been generously endowed by the religiousness of laymen over the centuries and it was only to be expected that Henry was anxious to lay claim to their treasures and supplement his lavish lifestyle.

Thomas Cromwell was appointed Vicar-General with authority to appoint Commissioners to visit every abbey and submit a report on their condition and especially upon their wealth. The purpose of the inspection was not to effect their reform but rather to find reasons for their closure, and Cromwell and his Commissioners ensured that such reports were secured. As a result, there followed the rampant destruction of much of the country's best architecture and art by vandals of the Reformation. Within six years, most of the nation's monasteries, religious houses and pilgrimage sites were dissolved and their treasures pillaged. Cromwell took great care to ensure that a portion of the spoils should find its way to him and into the hands of his relatives. The spoliation of the monasteries and collegiate churches was quickly followed by an attack on the parish church. Many of these contained considerable treasures such as silver plate, rich vestments and furniture.

The economic and political situation of the fourteenth and fifteenth centuries left their mark on the abbeys. Poverty had been a recurring problem to most since the Middle Ages. With the general reduction in the number of monks since the fourteenth century it was not surprising that there was a decline in the number of daily services, prayer and worship. When Henry VIII came to the throne in 1509, patronage and general assistance to the needy was on the wane and the monastic ideal had lost its appeal. The spiritual flame had been extinguished.

In 1536 an Act was passed for the dissolution of all monasteries and abbeys which were worth less that £200 a year, and all the Welsh abbeys fell into this category. One or two abbeys such as Strata Florida and Whitland gave monies to the crown in the hope that they could have been saved, but their position was only secured for a very short period of time – a doubtful privilege for their effort.

This appears to be the value of the abbeys at the time of their dissolution:

Monastery	Annual Value	Number of Monks
Tintern	£192	13
Valle Crucis	£188	6
Strata Marcella	£ 64	4
Glyn Nedd	£137	8
Whitland	£135	8
Strata Florida	£118	8
Cymer	£ 51	3
Cwm Hir	£ 28	3

It took no time at all to plunder the buildings: the lead from their roofs was stripped immediately and sold, and the bells and screens were also sold. The stone was used to build large houses in their vicinity and a detailed account of the destruction of the abbey at Maenan show that the stone was used to repair the castles at Caernarfon, Beaumaris and Harlech, and also the Treasury at Caernarfon:

The costs and charges that were done in taking
downe of the churche rouffe of the late Abbey of
Conweye and the kariage of stones and Tymbre from
the said Abbey to Caern
Imprimis payed to Thommas Hervey and Robert ap
Willm, carpenters by the space of vj days after the
Rate of vij the day unto ev'y of them ...   *vjs*
It'm payed to the same carpenters for their
Labour in taking down the said roufffe iiid a pese ...   *vijd*
It'm paide to Roberte ap John ap Atha for the
Freyght of his pykarfe of vij tone to carye
The said Tymbre by Water to Caer'n ...   *xijs*   *viiijd*
It'm payed for the ffreight of another
pykarde laden with stones of iiij tonne from
the said Abbey to Caer'n ...   *vs*   *iijd*

Similar accounts are available for other abbeys.

Early travellers to Wales took a great interest in the romantic monastic ruins and accounts of their visits make very interesting reading. One of those travellers was the Revd John Parker (1798–1860). He had a more sympathetic interest in Wales than most other travellers, and his numerous visits also gave him a much better knowledge of the country than any other visitor who may have made just one or two visits during the same period. He also expressed concern at the ruined state of the once magnificent buildings. Following a visit to Llanthony in 1843 he wrote in his journal:

> As an artist, I lament, and as a priest, although not a Romish one, I cannot behold a temple of God in ruins without pain and sorrow. No 'pictorial effect' can

compensate for the absence of worship or atone the crime of sacrilege. Every monastic ruin bears witness against the sin of those who destroyed His place of worship. I also visited the ruins of the dismantled house of Mr Landor, the absentee landlord of Llanthony. Is this another instance, I thought to myself, of the difficulties that beset the lay owners of church property? The materials of this house were obtained not only from neighbouring quarries but also from the central tower of Llanthony.

The Abbey of Cwm Hir, Radnorshire

When searching for a quiet and secluded spot to erect their abbey and live the monastic life, the Cistercians could not have found a more ideal site than at Cwm Hir by the river Clywedog in Radnorshire, not far from Rhayadr. Even today the site still retains the remoteness that was so important to the Cistercians. It was to Cwm Hir that the monks from Whitland went to establish their daughter foundation in 1143, and it was from there that monks went to Cymer near Dolgellau to establish yet another abbey there.

Although Cwm Hir is so remote, the Cistercians had their system of control, support and supervision for each abbey. Since the abbey had been established by the monks of Whitland, the Abbot of Whitland had the right and responsibility to visit, and similarly the Abbot of Cwm Hir in relation to the abbey of Cymer. In addition, every abbot of the order had to attend a meeting of the Chapter at Citeaux each year where the whole aspect of the work of the order would be discussed. This arrangement ensured that the rules of the order were kept. These annual visits to Citeaux had a great influence upon the architecture of the abbeys and, in general only very slight variations appear from their basic plan.

The abbey was established in 1143 by Maredudd ap Madog, Lord of Maelienydd. It was re-established in 1176 by Cadwaladr ap Madog and Einion Clyd, Lord of the Hundred of Elfael, and additional land was granted to it. These gifts, together with the gift of lands at Llangurig and Llanidloes in Montgomeryshire by Gwenwynwyn, were subsequently confirmed by the Charter of Edward II.

In many respects, the story of the abbey of Cwm Hir is a sad one as it was never properly completed, and if it had been, it would have been the largest and most magnificent abbey in the whole of Wales. There were fourteen bays in its nave, which measured 256 feet long and 80 feet wide, and there were twenty-six clustered columns, each with a distinctive carved capital.

In 1401 Owain Glyndŵr and his followers were in the vicinity. From there they were able to attack the English who had settled in Wales and also the Welsh who would not support his crusade. Montgomeryshire suffered badly from these attacks: the town of Montgomery was burnt, and also the area around Newtown. The abbey of Cwm Hir was also destroyed. There is no record of it being re-built and there is very little account of the abbey from that time until its dissolution in 1536. At that time only three monks remained. In 1538 the abbey came into the possession of John Turner, one of the King's men, and after twenty-five years the whole property was sold by the Crown to various landowners.

In 1542 the church at Llanidloes was being repaired and five of the columns of Cwm Hir were removed, to form an arcade to separate the nave from the northern aisle. The date 1542 has been carved on one of the numerous angels on the hammer-beams. In his book *Topographical Dictionary* Lewis states: 'an elegant screen from Abbey Cwmhir, formerly separated the chancel from the nave, but was removed in 1816 when the chancel and south aisle were rebuilt and not restored', but it is very unlikely that that screen was from Cwm Hir.

In 1644 the abbey was used as a garrison by Richard Fowler on behalf of the king. Only parts of the outer walls remain today as testimony to its past glory.

Following the abbey's destruction, the hamlet of Cwm Hir was left without a place of worship until 1680 when a small church, dedicated to the Virgin Mary, was erected in close proximity to the abbey, thus maintaining the connection with the Cistercians and the ancient abbey. Stones from the abbey were used for its construction. It was the invariable custom of the Cistercians to dedicate their abbeys to the Blessed Virgin Mary, and the dedication of the church at Cwm Hir, and many other churches so dedicated, bear witness to the influence of the Cistercians. In 1865 it was necessary to rebuild the church and this is the one to be seen at Cwm Hir today. Inside the church is a large stone which was once the lid of a coffin bearing the following inscription:

HIC JACET MABLI, CUJUS ANIMAE PROPITIETUR DEUS

[Here lies Mabli, on whose soul may God be merciful]

The style of the lettering on the lid suggests a period during Edward II's reign (1307–1327). This stone was discovered in 1827 by Mr Thomas Wilson, the then owner of the abbey, when he was excavating the site.

When the new church was being erected in 1865 it was the intention to incorporate a tympanum from the abbey over the doorway but unfortunately it broke when it was being

Some of the carvings that were moved from Abbey Cwm-hir to Cwm Hir Hall and other large houses nearby

transported there. This is now in the garden wall of Cwm Hir Farm. The carving on it is of the Transfiguration.

Mr Thomas Wilson, a businessman from London, had purchased the abbey in 1824 and started excavating the site. Another excavation took place in 1837; but sadly no reports exist. Wilson was not very willing to allow anyone on to the site because of some misunderstanding about tithes.

As can be seen from the photographs only a small portion of the walls remains today. But a memorial stone has been erected to Llywelyn ap Gruffydd, the last native Prince of Wales. There is a strong possibility that his headless body was buried within the precincts of the abbey. He had been killed near Builth Wells on Friday 11 December 1282.

Large numbers of carvings from the abbey were removed to the garden of Cwm Hir Hall and a few may be found in various other dwelling houses in the vicinity.

Strata Florida, Cardiganshire

By 1164, Whitland Abbey, under Norman patronage, was in a position to establish a daughter foundation in the Commote of Pennardd in Cardiganshire on the banks of the river Fflur – a site to this day referred to as '*yr hen fynachlog*' (the old monastery). Their stay there, however, was very short-lived as the monks found themselves at the mercy of both political and military events as the Welsh, according to the native chronicles *Brut y Tywysogion*, were 'united to throw off the rule of the French'.

Soon after establishing themselves at Strata Florida, the monks adopted the historical inheritance of the ancient Welsh church. The native Welsh *Annals*, previously kept at the ancient *clas* church at Llanbadarn Fawr, were to be continued in their Scriptorium which was to eclipse the work of the *clas* church. It was at Llanbadarn Fawr that Rhigyfarch wrote *The Life of St David*.

When the Revd John Parker visited the site in 1836 he referred to:

> this inviting spot, interesting alike to the historian, to the painter and the poet. Here in times of warlike violence dwelt the man of learning and the man of taste. He dwelt here who scrutinised the mysterious dealings of God with a Celtic nation, he who recorded amid the silence of contemplation the fall of heroes and the strivings of mighty men. He dwelt here who held with his hands the precious manuscripts, the ritual of the apostolic British church.

In its turn Strata Florida established a daughter abbey at Llantarnan in 1179 and at Rhedynogfelen near Caernarfon in 1186. Their stay at Rhedynogfelen was very short before they were re-established at Aberconwy.

Whitland became the mother abbey of Cwm Hir in 1176 and Cwm Hir in 1198 became the mother abbey of Cymer near Dolgellau. In 1170 the abbey of Strata Marcella near Welshpool was established; it was from there that monks were sent out in 1201 to establish the abbey of Valle Crucis near Llangollen. The Cistercians thus became firmly established in north Wales and had considerable influence in the area.

In 1184, the Lord Rhys granted a charter to the monks of Strata Florida confirming the grants which he had already given them and at the same time granting additional lands, thus ensuring its considerable success. It grew from strength to strength and continued its allegiance to its benefactor; in its grounds a number of princes of south Wales were buried. It was at Strata Florida that Llywelyn the Great held his historic council of war with the Welsh chieftains when they were calling their forces to resist the English king.

Despite its success, it was also to experience troubled times; it was attacked during the wars of Edward I, and in 1284 it was burnt for the second time when struck by lightning. The Black Death (1338–1349) claimed the lives of a large number of monks and it is estimated that it claimed the lives of half of the population of the country, opening a new chapter in its economic history. The monks supported the resurrection of Owain Glyndŵr, and as a result the abbey was possessed by the king in 1402 and the monks were thrown out. It enjoyed but little success afterwards.

There were at times problems of misbehaviour. In 1195 some of the lay brethren were called to Citeaux to be disciplined because they had visited the abbey of Cwm Hir in a drunken state and made a nuisance of themselves. As a result of this, the Chapter at Citeaux ruled that beer should not be drunk in the abbey granges in Wales and only water was permitted. It does not appear, however, that much attention was given to the order because in the following year the Abbot of Whitland had to visit Strata Florida because of further misdemeanours by the lay brethren. He ruled that no new brethren were to be admitted until total abstinence had been achieved. In 1503 one of the monks was convicted of making counterfeit coins!

The following account appears in a manuscript of 1295 after the abbey had been burnt:

Stone carvings in Strata Florida

The Abbot of Strata Florida foolishly pronounced the King that on a certain day and at a certain time, he would bring the County of Cardigan into amity with the King, but when the King with an armed force was waiting for a very long time, no one of the Welshmen came to the appointed spot. Therefore, the King said 'Burn, Burn' and so the fire which never cries out 'enough' in like manner wrapped both the Abbey and the County in flame.

With the dissolution of the abbey its treasures were scattered, together with its furniture and all its carvings, and in the ruins lay the tombs of the Welsh princes.

Valle Crucis, Denbighshire

The ruins of Valle Crucis Abbey lie a few miles from Llangollen, and like all other Cistercian abbeys it is situated in one of the most beautiful areas in Wales. The site reflects perfectly the monastic ideal for a settlement 'far from the concourse of men'. Not far from the abbey is the ninth-century pillar of Eliseg, which was erected by Cyngen, son of Cadell, prince of Powys, to commemorate his grandfather Elise. It is the stonemason's error which accounts for 'Eliseg'.

The abbey was established in 1201 by Madog ap Gruffudd Maelor, ruler of north Powys, and thirteen monks from the abbey of Strata Marcella, near Welshpool, came to settle here.

The abbey possessed considerable tracts of land. By the middle of the thirteenth century the revenue from their sheep accounted for a sizeable part of their income, but their real wealth came from the tithes of surrounding parishes – amounting to 75 per cent of their total assets. It could well be that they concentrated too much on their financial position whilst disregarding their spiritual responsibilities, for within a year the Abbot was accused of seldom celebrating the Mass. Another complaint early in its history was that women were allowed to enter the abbey.

In 1274 the abbot was one of seven Cistercian abbots who wrote to the Pope in support of Llywelyn ap Gruffudd because the Bishop of St Asaph had brought a complaint against him. Consequently, the abbey and its lands became ready prey in the Wars of Edward I.

By the end of the thirteenth century Valle Crucis achieved importance in the history of Welsh Literature, because it was here that *Brut y Tywysogion* (the very early chronicle of the Welsh princes) was kept from 1282–1332.

In 1535 Valle Crucis was to suffer the same fate as all the other abbeys of Wales at the hands of Henry VIII and only six monks were there at its dissolution. The silver communion vessels were either sold or sent to London for smelting. Their other treasures were also sold and some of their bells were sent to churches in Shropshire. Sir William Pickering became the abbey's owner, but under the terms of his lease the lead from the roof had to be given to the Crown. Once that had been done, the building could only fall into ruin and for centuries the stones from its walls were taken away and part of the abbey became a farmhouse. By the eighteenth century only ruins remained as testimony to a once proud abbey.

A tomb slab, discovered in front of the high altar commemorates Madog ap Gruffudd – a great-grand-son of the founder of the abbey – and can be seen there today.

Chapter 3

The pilgrims

Stand at the crossroads and look.
Ask for the ancient paths
Ask where the good way is.
In addition, walk in it,
And you will find rest for your souls.

Jeremiah 6:16

Pilgrimages have always played an important part in the history of Christianity from its very beginning, as indeed in other religions. Neither the distances to be covered nor the dangers encountered on the way posed any obstacles. It was the power of the Church and its sacraments, together with the intercession of the saints, that paved the way to salvation for the Christians. The power of the Virgin Mary and the saints, especially local saints, had a profound influence on religion. The relics associated with them, such as their bones (authentic or imaginary), their bells, crosiers, altars, wells and books, became powerful objects and merited the greatest reverence. Belief in the relics was central to the pilgrims and they inspired the medieval faithful with a sense of power and mystery. Such was the importance placed upon pilgrimages that if a man was too sick to undertake the journey for himself it was common to employ a proxy to do the journey in his place.

A study of the wells remaining today provides an insight into the beliefs and confidence of the people before the days of Christianity and will show how important they were to the pilgrims. They proved useful to the early Christians for baptising their members, and some wells were reported to have had curative powers. These ancient wells were associated with the early saints; large numbers of them were associated with the Virgin Mary. The fact that the population was largely illiterate made it easy for superstition to gain ground. Belief in supernatural powers was often attached to the religious relics from the fifth to the fifteenth centuries, and was an essential element in pilgrimages. Pilgrimages were seen as the means of salvation, they were undertaken conscientiously, and it was necessary to display true Christian virtue.

The aim of the early pilgrims was to visit those sites associated with important episodes in the Christian faith, and particularly where Christ was born and where he was crucified.

Pilgrimages were as important in Wales as in any other country. Pope Calixtus II decreed that two pilgrimages to St David's in Pembrokeshire were equal to one to Rome, and that three pilgrimages there were equivalent to one to Jerusalem.

The pilgrimage to St David's was of particular importance to the Welsh. Bishop Barlow, on the other hand, referred to the place as 'a hotbed of superstition and idolatry'. Such was his objection to the fact that thousands of pilgrims visited the place that at one time he had it in mind to establish his cathedral at Carmarthen. He considered St David's to be 'a delicate daughter of Rome, naturally resembling her mother in shameless confusion, and like qualified with other perverse properties of execrable malignity'.

Nowhere was considered too far for a pilgrimage. Giraldus Cambrensis mentioned that during his visit to Rome he met there a number of pilgrims from his own country.

The period from the middle of the fifteenth century up to the Reformation was a period when great expenditure was lavished on the churches and many of them were rebuilt, extended or decorated. This was the people's way of showing their pride in their places of worship. Painted glass windows showing biblical scenes were incorporated, and sometimes, a 'Jesse window' would be inserted showing the lineage of Christ from Jesse. The inspiration for this concept comes from the prophecy of Isaiah, chapter 11, verse 1: 'There shall come forth a rod out of the stem of Jesse, and a branch shall grow out of his roots'. The most outstanding example of such a window is to be found in St Dyfnog's church, Llanrhaeadr-yng-Nghinmeirch. The period also saw the construction of rood lofts and screens. Wales has some outstanding examples of such screens intricately carved in a variety of patterns and designs, although many such screens were lost during the Reformation. Over the screen would be a carving of the crucified Christ with the Virgin Mary on one side and St John on the other. The pilgrims' offerings would have contributed towards their cost in a number of instances.

Christ's suffering during his last days was of great significance and this is borne out in the carvings both in stone and in wood. The rood screen became important structures in many of the small churches in rural Wales and they attracted a number of pilgrims to places like Llangynwyd, Penrhys, Llanbeblig, Llaneilian, Rhuddlan and Tremeirchion. The ancient Welsh Bard Hywel Dafydd wrote an ode to the 'Golden Rood at Brecon Priory': here the pilgrims would see the Virgin Mary on the Rood Loft smiling at them at times, and at other times she would be seen crying – such was their faith and superstition.

The Church itself would contribute to the pilgrim movement by extolling the value of the relics and the reverence that was due to them, together with the fact that their sins would be forgiven. Pilgrimages were sometimes imposed as a punishment and penance on the people. A constant flow of pilgrims to a particular church would increase the church's financing – not forgetting, of course, the sale of indulgences. It was not until 1536 that reverence for relics and the sale of indulgences was forbidden, and this caused much concern in a number of areas. It was the attitude of the bishops and priests that would ultimately determine whether such an edict was successful or not. By 1538, however, it was necessary to issue a further order forbidding the people 'to repose their trust in wanderings and pilgrimages, offer of money, candles or tapers to images or relics, or kissing or licking the same, or saying over a number of beads not understood or minded on'. It has been suggested the orders had little effect in Wales because the people did not understand English.

These prohibitions, and the fact that the people could not offer prayers for the dead, was a severe blow to ordinary men and women because it meant that they had lost a very valuable support in their very hard lives. These things had been so important in their lives for generations, and they were most reluctant to forego them.

A pilgrimage to Bardsey island off the coast of Caernarfonshire was always popular, and remains so to this day, with the Bishop of Bangor still arranging occasional pilgrimages there. On their way to Bardsey, they would have visited the grave of St Beuno in his church at Clynnog. One visitor in 1589 expressed concern at what he saw there:

the abominable idolatries, the sacrifice of bullocks to Saint Beuno; the open carrying of rosaries by the church people who claimed to read them as well as others can read a book; calling on saints or idols to help them in all extremities and above all, the sign of the cross was almost superstitiously made among them abused – when closing windows, leaving livestock in the fields and burying their dead.

These superstitions were still alive in 1783 when Thomas Pennant made his tour of north Wales, and he wrote:

in the midst is the tomb of the saint, plain and altar-shaped. Votaries were wont to have great faith in him and did not doubt that by means of a single night's lodging on his tomb, a cure would be found of all diseases. It was customary to cover it with rushes, and leave on it till morning sick children after making them first undergo ablution in the neighbouring holy well, and I myself saw on it a feather bed, on which a poor paralytic boy from Merionethshire had lain on it the whole night, after undergoing the same ceremony.

From Clynnog the pilgrims would proceed past Aelhaearn's well, and above Nant Gwytheyrn they would receive food and shelter in accommodation specially prepared for them. They would then have visited the little church at Pistyll, where at one time there was a large herb garden that the pilgrims would have found most useful. Herbs are strewn on the church floor to this day. At Pistyll there was a farmhouse free from the payment of tithes for as long as the pilgrims were welcomed there. From there they would proceed to Nefyn and on to Aberdaron, whence they would cross to Bardsey. This was the sacred place for all pilgrims. It was from Aberdaron that Pennant crossed to Bardsey, and on his journey over he noticed that 'the mariners seemed tinctured with piety of the place, for they neither had not rowed far, but they made a full stop, pulled off their hats, and offered a short prayer'. Bardsey remains to this day as charismatic as it was for the early pilgrims, with the legend of 20,000 saints who are reputed to be buried there.

Pennant Melangell

Pennant Melangell Church c. 1830

Some of the Pilgrims' paths are as popular today as they were in the twelfth century, with the number of pilgrims increasing

Cwm Hir Abbey today

*Clustered columns from Cwm Hir Abbey
in the arcade of Llanidloes church*

49

Vale Crucis Abbey, 1779

Romanesque shrine in Pennant Melangell church

Pennant Melangell screen after its restoration

Llanbister, Radnor

Llanbister, Radnor

'Derfel's horse' at Llandderfel church

Detail of screen at Llandderfel church

Section of the screen at Nant Peris

Llanaelhaearn

53

Fan vaulting in the screen at Conwy church

Section of the screen at Conwy showing an Eagle's claw holding a fish
– and a Pomegranate – the badge of Katherine of Aragon

Siwan, wife of Llywelyn Fawr – her stone coffin at Beaumaris church

Misericord at Beaumaris church

A pelican feeding its young with its own blood

*Ruins of St Mary's Church,
Newtown*

*John Parker's drawings of sections
of the Newtown screen
as it was in 1829*

*Section of the screen at St David's church, Newtown
removed from St Mary's church*

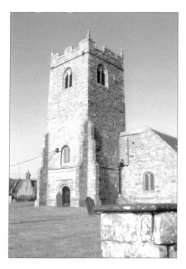

Llanengan church in Llŷn

Detail of one of Llanengan's screens

One of two screens at Llanengan church

The screen at Llanwnnog showing the entrance to the chancel

Section of the Llanwnnog screen showing the two-headed 'Amphisbaena' – a symbol of the Middle Ages

Screen at Llanegryn church with closer looks at some details

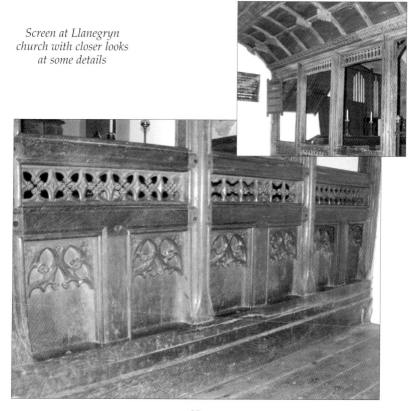

59

Llywelyn Fawr's stone cask at Llanrwst

Section of the screen at Llanrwst

Llaneilian church, Anglesey

Painting of a skeleton on the ceiling of Llaneilian church

Screen at Llaneilian church

Penmon priory and church

Bugeildy, Radnor

Screen at Clynnog church after its restoration in 1856

Screen at St Issui's church, Patrico

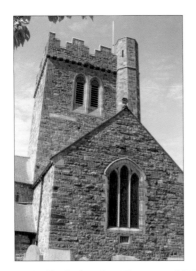

Cadfan's church at Tywyn, and 'Maen Cadfan' – a stone pillar with the earliest example of Welsh inscription

Rhulen, Radnor

almost every year. One such site is Pennant Melangell, where the church of St Melangell (*Monacella*) is located amidst the beautiful surroundings of the vale of Tanat high in the Berwyn Mountains. It is interesting to note that this church has always been regarded as a pilgrims' church; the actual parish church is situated in the village of Llangynog.

The history of this church is very similar to that of many other rural churches in Wales. In 1987, a considerable amount of work was required if it was to be saved from destruction. The position was so serious that it was decided to remove the roof and then leave it to the elements to do their worse. But in the face of considerable opposition it was possible to save the building. Between 1988 and 1992 restoration was carried out and the church of St Melangell stands today as a treasure in the inimitable beauty of the vale of Tanat, and its future is secure for future generations to enjoy the same piece of mind as the early pilgrims must have enjoyed after their visit and services are being held there.

The first reference to St Melangell's church is to be found in the Norwich Taxatio c.1254, which gives it value at £1.40. By 1291 the Lincoln Taxatio shows its value at just over £10. Possibly the reason for this was the increasing popularity of the cult of Melangell resulting in the ever-increasing number of pilgrims making their way there. By the 1660s its value was down once again – no doubt because of the Reformation.

Archaeological excavations have confirmed that there had been a church on the site since the twelfth century. Many churches were built in this area at about the same time, such as those at Llanyblodwel, Llansantffraid-ym-Mechain, Llanfechain, Llanfair Caereinon and Meifod, to name but a few.

65

These churches also retain some twelfth-century features.

Inside St Melangell's church is to be found one of the oldest surviving Romanesque shrines in Europe.

After the days of Henry VIII the cult of Melangell came under fierce threat and in 1561 the Bishop of St Asaph issued an Order: 'that every and each of them [priests] shall forthwith ... remove and put away all and every fayned relyque within their several churches and abolyshe ther aulters yn the same, within eight days'. However, when an image is destroyed so also is its meaning, and this proved a great loss to the pilgrims.

It is reasonable, therefore, to assume that this was the time when the shrine of Melangell was removed and that her tomb in the little chapel, or oratory, was closed up. The room is still called 'Cell y Bedd' (the cell of the grave). By the end of the seventeenth century parts of the shrine had been used to repair the lych gate and parts of the church walls.

Between 1989 and 1992 the apse at the eastern end of the church was reconstructed and Melangell's shrine was re-erected behind the altar.

Although we know very little about Melangell herself, one aspect of her life has been handed down to us in folklore and related by W. A. Griffiths in *Tales from Welsh History and Romance* (1915):

> In the year 604, according to an old monkish manuscript, King Brochwel Yscythriog was indulging in his favourite pastime in the Vale of Tanat, and his greyhounds had started a hare. The king and his huntsmen followed in hot pursuit. In the narrow vale of Pennant the hare disappeared into a thick bramble thicket, followed by the dogs. The king eagerly dashed after them, and to his

surprise found a most lovely girl kneeling in devout prayers with the hare lying in the folds of her garments, boldly facing the dogs. Indifferent to her presence, the king urged on his dogs, but the more he urged them the more they howled and slunk away. Even the horn of his huntsman became stuck to his lips. Thereupon, King Brochwel realised that he was in the presence of no ordinary person so asked the maiden what her name was and how long she had lived there. The maiden replied that she was Monacella, the daughter of King Iochwel of Ireland, and that she had fled from her father's court rather than marry the man for whom she was destined. She had accordingly, hidden, under the protection of God, among the Berwyn mountains, living in a rocky cave and passing the days in prayer and meditation. Whereupon King Brochwel, being greatly impressed by her beauty and anxious for her safety, gave her the portion of land adjoining her cell, commanding it to be a sanctuary land, which no man should violate upon pain of death. For thirty-seven years the virgin Monacella lived here in peace and security and all the hares became like tame animals, following her about like lambs. She also established a small nunnery for virgins who devoted themselves entirely to the service of prayer.

For centuries, few people would kill a hare on the sanctuary land and hares in the neighbourhood were known as '*wyn bach Melangell*' (the lambs of Monacella).

An old parish register contains the following words:

Mil engyl a Melangell
Trechant lu fyddin y fall.

(St Monacella and her thousand angels
Shall triumph over the whole power of hell)

However, despite all the other treasures that are to be found in this church, the screen, dating from the fifteenth century, must remain the most important. It has been moved around and damaged over the centuries, and was placed in its present position in 1991.

In 1837 the Revd John Parker visited Pennant Melangell and gave a detailed description of the screen as it was at that time, together with an accurate drawing. In view of the damage which has occurred over the years since his visit, it is important to give Parker's description in full as it was at the time of his visit:

> In the casement mouldings, the legend of St Melangell is represented. The cleverness and ingenuity with which the story is told, in spite of the trammels imposed upon the artist by the requirements of the running border, are deserving of attention. The various figures, although carved in equally strong relief, and occupying equal intervals of the branch work and foliage in a running border, are nevertheless at five several distances in point of size. There is no grouping, the workmanship is minute, but rather grotesque, and the different animals are more or less out of drawing. They are painted red and pink and white, the tracery panels under them alternately red and blue, the leading members of some pale colour, the branch work and the foliage are also of light colour,

but the chromatic decorations are much faded, and there is not light enough to ascertain them. One tracery panel has its gouge work painted red, the next blue, that at the next one red, and so on alternatively. The screen itself, on the rood loft of which the above formed a cornice or frieze, remain in its position between the chancel and the nave. It comprised four compartments on each side of the doorway, or entrance, which is just double the width of the side divisions; the spandrels are filled with tracery of the same design and are of the fourteenth century character. Scenes on the border trail are (i) Brochwel Ysgythrog, the Prince of Powys on horseback with a sword in his right hand; (ii) Half kneeling huntsman trying in vain to remove the horn which he was raising to his lips for the purpose of blowing it, when it remained fast and could not be sounded; (iii) Melangell represented as an Abbess on a cushion, her left hand grasping a foliated crosier; (iv) the hunted hare scattering towards the figure of the saint. The hare is painted red; (v) a greyhound in pursuit with its leg entangled among the branches of the running border. The dog is painted red of a pale colour; (vi) a nondescript animal, intended, I suppose for a dog.

The importance of Parker's description of the screen is that it gives a unique indication of the original colours that were later covered with many layers of dark varnish at the hands of Victorian restorers. Parts of the figures have also been lost since Parker's days.

It is also interesting to note that carvings of the hare have been found on ancient graves at Valle Crucis and in the churchyards at Llanyblodwel, St Asaph and Ysbyty Ifan. The hare was a popular figure in Celtic religion.

Despite everything that has happened to this screen over the centuries it is still regarded an unique treasure amongst the churches of Wales.

St Derfel's Church, Llandderfel

Merionethshire also had a special appeal for the early pilgrims because in the church at Llandderfel, near Bala, stood the image of Derfel Gadarn.

In 1538, Bishop William Barlow was proud of the fact that he had destroyed a candle in Hereford which, according to the beliefs of the superstitious, would burn forever. At the same time, Dr Ellis Prys, one of Thomas Cromwell's officers, was acting just as thoroughly at Llandderfel. He wrote to his master that he had removed the image of Derfel Gadarn – the image which had sustained the pilgrims for generations.

In the 1530s the success of the Reformation in Merionethshire as in all other areas of Wales, was largely dependent upon local factors. The Diocese of St Asaph was staunchly Catholic in the sixteenth century, and Protestantism – the new religion – had to fight hard to gain recognition over superstition and the old order. This is not surprising since Wales saw the Reformation as an English imposition. It was difficult for the people to accept the loss of devotional practices which had been in place for centuries. The language also posed additional difficulties. There was an urgent need for the people of Wales to be provided with literature in their native language, and it was the publication of the Welsh Bible in 1588 that was to herald a new era.

Owain Glyndŵr's uprising had caused much destruction in Wales and a number of churches, as well as cathedrals, were damaged. However, the second half of the fifteenth century experienced a revival of interest in church life, and churches up and down the country were either repaired or completely rebuilt. This was also the time when some of our most outstanding screens were erected and many of them, including the one at Llandderfel, are still standing to this day. In the wake of such revival, pilgrimages to the rood screen at Chester, St Winifred's Well and Derfel's image, for example, were part of this pattern.

We know very little about Derfel Gadarn. Tradition has it that he was buried at Bardsey, but we do know for certain that pilgrimages to his shrine at Llandderfel were very popular just before the Reformation. It was claimed that he could cure both people and animals. When Dr Ellis Prys visited Llandderfel in 1538 the pilgrims' offerings brought substantial wealth to the church. The priest and the parishioners offered Dr Prys £40 if he would save the image – a considerable amount at that time. In the early 1500s repairs were carried out to the church and the pilgrims' offerings would have contributed substantially towards the cost.

An important virtue attributed to the image was that it could save souls from hell-fire, and because of this hundreds of pilgrims would visit it daily with their offerings of cattle, oxen, horses and cash, although it has been suggested that the animals would have been brought to be blessed and cured rather than as offerings. As many as 500–600 pilgrims had visited the church on 5 April 1538 – the day before Dr Prys wrote to Thomas Cromwell:

that notwithstanding there ys an image of Dervelgadarn within the saide diocese, in whome the people have so great confidence, hope and trusts, that they comme dayly a pilgrimage unto hym, some with money, in so much ther was five or syxe hyndrethe pilgrims to a mans estimacion to the said Image the fifth daie of this presente monthe of Aprill. The innocente people hathe been sore allured and enticed to worshippe the said image, that who so ever will offer anie thinge to the said Image of Dervellgadarn he hath power to fetch hyhm or them that so offers oute of Hell wen they be damped. Therefore, for the reformacion and amendmente of the premises, I would gladlie know by this berer your honourable pleasure and will, as knowith God, who ever preserve your Lordshipe longe in welthe and honor. Written in Northe Wales the vj days of this present Aprill.

Your bedman and dahyle orator by dutie.
Elis Price

Thomas Cromwell's unequivocal order to Dr Prys was that the image was to be taken down and sent to London. For his part Dr Prys was only too happy to conform to his master's order. In a letter dated 28 April 1538 he wrote that he had been offered £40 by the parishioners to save the image, but that he would gladly sent it to London, and in May it was burnt publicly at Smithfield – together with the friar, Brother Forest, one of Catherine of Aragon's confessors, who had refused to accept Henry VIII's supremacy. Some people saw this as fulfilling the prophecy that some day Derfel Gadarn 'would set a whole forest on fire'.

Despite the removal of the image and a host of other images throughout Wales, pilgrimages were still important. The dissolution of the monasteries, together with the destruction of images once glorified and cherished, meant that the new religion was intent upon destroying once and for all everything which the people had considered important, if not sacrosanct, in their lives. Although the image of Derfel himself was taken to London to be burnt, his horse is still to be seen in the porch of his church at Llandderfel, demonstrating both the strength of feeling and the superstition of the early pilgrims.

Derfel's horse, however, is not the only treasure to be found in this church, for here also is a screen from the end of the fifteenth century. Originally there was a seat in each bay of the screen, and the owners of these seats had the right of burial under them. If a coffin had been used for burial then a period of sixteen years had to elapse before another burial could take place there, but if a coffin had not been used then the period was reduced to eight years. The beam at the base of the screen was referred to as '*y pren pymtheg*' (the 15-foot beam) referring to the length of the chancel. Sixty people could have been accommodated in the rood loft, but at the end of the eighteenth century the loft was removed and its upper portion was used to form the front of a gallery at the western end of the church. Fortunately, the architect responsible for subsequent alterations to the church reinstated the section over the screen once again. Flowers and vine leaves have been skilfully carved on its western side. There are twenty-five panels above the screen. The eastern side has not been as skilfully carved as the western side, but when the rood loft was in place that side would not have been visible. Roman numerals have been carved on the panels but they are not in the correct order – could it be that the panels have been wrongly replaced at one time or are they the marks of the ancient craftsmen?

St Winifred's Well, Holywell

A number of wells in Wales were associated with the pilgrims and many of them are still important today.

In 1774, Dr Johnson and Mrs Hester Lynch Thrale were on a visit to north Wales. Mrs Thrale had inherited Bachegraig in Denbighshire and she was anxious to view her inheritance. On 3 April of that year they were both at St Winifred's Well, but Dr Johnson was not very impressed, and his main concern was that 'a woman bathed while we all looked on'. Mrs Thrale for her part expressed quite different concern, because:

> we saw the devastation committed by Puritanism, which in its zeal had battered poor St Winifred and displaced her statue, broken three of the columns surrounding the well which had any effigies upon them, and left nothing but the stone at the bottom of the water which bears any mark of ancient superstition and is spotted with red in two or three places, and the Roman Catholics believe from their hearts that it was stained by the blood of their favourite Virgin Mary.

According to tradition, Caradog, a Welsh prince in the seventh century, was walking in the area when he came across Winifred working in a field not far from her Uncle Beuno. Caradog requested food and water from her, but when he tried to seduce her Winifred tried to run towards her uncle for safety; Caradog ran after her and cut off her head, 'which falling to earth, deserved of God to have a fountain of water spring in the place, which to this day continueth. When Beuno saw that the head had come to rest near the church wall he cursed Caradog so that the ground swallowed him up. Beuno joined the head back with the body and Winifred survived for fifteen years, with only a small scar showing on her neck.

An unknown monk wrote down Winifred's legend only in the twelfth century. Dr William Fleetwood, Bishop of St Asaph, was against the pilgrimage to her well in his diocese, stating that he could not believe a story recorded 500 years after the incident. The tale of a severed head miraculously rejoined to a body occurs several times in Celtic mythology.

A substantial building erected towards the end of the fifteenth century stands at her well and modern-day pilgrims still believe that its waters can cure them. The pilgrimage to St Winifred's well is the only pilgrimage to have survived unchecked through the Reformation, demonstrating the strength of the Roman Catholic faith. The well is the most complete medieval shrine in Britain.

The well cult denotes the reverence which the people felt was due to these ancient wells. Before the days of Christianity, wells, lakes and rivers were often regarded as gods, with special ceremonies and offerings were being made to them. Do not the wells of today have a special significance to us? And is this not shown by our habit of throwing coins into them in the hope that it will bring us good luck?

The Church's attitude was demonstrated by the order of St Augustine when he transformed the ancient pagan sites 'into a Christian solemnity' and their ancient worshipping places into churches. The sacrifice of animals could continue but as 'Christian banquets for the praise of God'. Although he wanted to destroy pagan images Augustine was prepared to purify ancient temples with holy water from the wells. Altars were to be erected in them, 'converted from the worship of devils to the worship of the true God'.

The continuity of the site was maintained and the new God was to be installed. It is not surprising, therefore, that wells remained popular with the pilgrims and that their offerings would provide material benefits such as contributing towards the fine Jesse window at Llanrhaeadr, which was completed in 1535. Water from wells was used for baptism and is still used in a number of churches to this day.

Before Henry VIII inaugurated a new era in British religious life he had made more than one pilgrimage to the well of Our Lady of Walsingham in Norfolk, and like other pilgrims, he walked the last two miles bare-footed. In a letter written about 1590 it was said of the Welsh people:

> They doe still goe in heaps on pilgrimages to the wonted wells and places of superstition; and in the nightes after the feasts when the ould offerings were used to be kept at anie chappell, albeit the church be pulled down, yet doe they come to the place where the church or chappell was, by great journeys barefooted.

Mr Francis Jones, in his book *The Holy Wells of Wales*, reports that at least 437 wells bear the names of saints and a further sixty-five wells are associated with Christian practices in Wales.

However, it was not always good deeds that were associated with wells, and some were used for cursing and sorcery in order to occasion maximum harm. Elian's Well at Old Colwyn was such a well. It was reported that the woman who looked after this well at the end of the eighteenth century made about £300 a year from it. This well attracted such notoriety that the rector of the parish had to take steps to fill it up, but it was said that it was secretly used for cursing as late as 1871.

Chapter 4

The years 1500–1800

(i) Henry VIII and the Reformation

The Reformation was not a conscious and natural progression in the history of the Church, nor a revolt against Roman Catholicism in England, but rather the result of the Pope's procrastination concerning 'the King's Great Matter' – the dissolution of Henry VIII's marriage to Catherine of Aragon. The result of this was the repudiation of Papal authority, and a number of Acts of Parliament in 1534 severed all financial, judicial and administrative links with Rome. In the words of Thomas Cromwell, Henry would become the richest prince in Christendom.

Without thinking, Henry turned Catholic Britain into a Protestant nation. The Act of Supremacy of 1534 confirmed Henry and his successors as 'the only supreme head on earth of the Church of England'.

In 1536 and again in 1539 Acts were passed for the dissolution of the monasteries, and in 1538 religious shrines were to be taken down, relics destroyed and treasures to be confiscated. In 1547, the year of Henry's death, several traditional ceremonies of the medieval church were abolished and a further Order made for the removal of any remaining images. Because of this, wall paintings were lime-washed. Quite unintentionally, this preserved quite a few of them; some are being rediscovered today for the first time when repairs and alterations are carried out in the churches.

However, despite the break from Rome, Henry adhered to his Catholic faith and was against any major changes. It was only after his death in 1547 that Protestantism became the official religion and the Book of Common Prayer was used for the first time in 1549.

When Edward VI succeeded his father in 1547, his Commissioners instructed that confiscated church treasures were to be sold and the proceeds sent to the Exchequer. Inventories at the time show that St John's church, Cardiff, lost 'its ornaments, three copes of red velvet, a chasuble of the same suit, a cope of blue velvet, two copes of red damask and one cope of satin'. It was only the easily moveable treasures that were taken – the removal of the rest was to follow later. Orders, as late as 1583 provided for the removable of ornaments, which had not been removed previously.

In 1587, John Penry of Brecon, writing about conditions in Wales, demonstrated that the changes brought about by the Reformation had not, by then, penetrated the lives of the ordinary people. They did not understand the new Book of Common Prayer or the New Testament translated into Welsh by William Salesbury in 1567. Their beliefs were governed by much earlier rites and ceremonies of the Church. Prayers were still offered to images and the saints invoked. The people believed that they would only be saved 'at the entreaty of the Virgin Mary who shall desire her Son, after judgement given, to save as many of the damned as may be covered under her mantle'.

When Mary became Queen in 1553, she set out to return England to the Catholic faith. A series of persecution of Protestants commenced, and she became known as 'Bloody

Mary'. It was also directed that the Latin Mass was to be celebrated and paintings were to be restored. The extreme beliefs of her followers, together with the unpopularity of her marriage to Philip of Spain, militated against her aims.

Upon Mary's death in 1558 and the succession of Elizabeth I to the throne, the resurrection of the Catholic church was doomed and the Anglican church was established on firm foundations. The first Book of Common Prayer, authorised by the Act of Uniformity in 1549, was revised following Protestant criticism, and a second version was issued in 1552–53 – although, with the accession of Queen Mary, it was never brought into use. The 1552 version established Protestantism in England and confirmed the distinction between the Mass and the Communion, and it was reissued in 1559 in a slightly amended form. A weekly penalty was also imposed on those refusing to attend church.

However, Wales was loath to accept Protestantism, as it gave no reason for changing the old faith, and there was little inducement to give up the Latin Mass for an English one that was not understood either. The English Prayer Book was generally as unintelligible as the Latin service, and it had no sentimental attachments.

When Dr Nickolas Robinson became Bishop of Bangor in 1566, he worked diligently against Catholicism. When he came to his diocese, he wrote:

> I have found since I came to this country images and altars standing in church un-defaced, lewd and indecent vigils and watches observed, much pilgrimage going, many candles set up in honour of saints and some relics yet carried about, and all the country full of beads and

knots, besides divers other monuments of wilful serving of God.

Other reports disclose that in Wales the people ordinarily carried their beads about with them in church and used them in prayers. Perhaps it is not surprising that the success of the Reformation was only slowly accepted in Wales.

The sixteenth century saw unprecedented changes in the religious life of the country when ancient customs were forbidden. This was also the time when parishes were established as units of local government and increasing responsibilities placed upon the shoulders of the wardens, and priests were urging their parishioners to contribute towards helping the poor. Ultimately, this was to lead to some overseers of the poor becoming very powerful and operating in a way that was detrimental to those they were supposed to help. Parish registers will give numerous examples of their actions. The line between diligence and officiousness was often very thin.

In 1550, an Order was made for the removal of the old stone altars. Communion tables were to be set up in the chancel so that the communicants could approach them from either side. When the church at Llansilyn was repaired in 1890 part of the old stone altar with two carved crosses on it was discovered under the floor of the chancel. It now forms the sill of the window nearest to the altar.

With the republication of the Common Prayer Book in 1552, many old customs were discontinued, together with certain vestments and superstitious images that had not been removed. What we see in most churches today is just a shadow of what they would have been like.

Following the extreme measures taken during Mary's short

reign, steps were taken to reconcile the various factions within the Church and a number of restrictions were imposed to ensure that the extremists would never again be able to impose their rule.

The screen dividing the chancel from the nave was allowed to remain in position but the rood was to be removed. The rood loft itself, which in the late medieval Church had often accommodated a choir, was allowed to remain. Reformers frowned upon these choirs, which had performed the elaborate music of the period, and congregational singing was encouraged. In some churches, the rood loft was removed and re-erected at the western end of the church for the use of the choir. The Communion Table was to be kept against the eastern wall so that the narrow ends faced east and west thus enabling the communicants to kneel at all four sides.

As the people became more literate, the Creed, Ten Commandments and the Lord's Prayer were painted on the walls in place of the paintings which had been removed.

(ii) 1600–1700

Despite the considerable changes which had occurred immediately after the Reformation, the parish church still remained an important centre of the community both for religious and cultural purposes, but it was a different kind of church. Regular attendance at church services were obligatory and absentees punished. Under the Act of Uniformity 1559:

> All and every person and persons inhabiting within this realm or any other of the Queen's dominions, shall report to the parish church ... upon every Sunday and other days ordained and use to be kept as Holy Days, and

then and there to abide orderly and soberly during the time of Common Prayer, preaching or other service of God there to be used or ministered.

It was very difficult to ensure that the provisions of the Act were kept in remote areas, and amongst the poor, although the old and infirm were excused, together with those who had no suitable clothing.

Enforcing attendance meant that the whole community would meet in the church, thus enabling problems of the day to be discussed and resolved, and old quarrels settled. This sometimes involved individuals fighting each other, and some churches would have appointed wardens to maintain order – and also to patrol the church during services, tapping on the head with a long staff those who might have fallen asleep.

Penance was still a common occurrence in the seventeenth century. Having to do public penance in church on Sundays was considered very offensive, especially to women, who were more often required to do penance than men. It is no surprise, therefore, that those who could afford to do so paid a fine rather than submit themselves to public ridicule.

At this time, the altar was not the main focal point of the church as the pulpit and preaching became more important. The liturgical changes effected by the Reformation resulted in greater emphasis being placed on direct communication between the priest and the congregation. As a result, seats were arranged so as to face the pulpit and box pews became popular. There was great competition between the more wealthy families to secure the best seats, which became the symbol of their importance and standing in the community. Some families would transfer their seats in their wills to others of their family.

During the Civil War of 1642–1649 both the Church and Monarchy were considered to be enemies of the state. Iconoclasm and desecration were rife. Churches were plundered, stained glass windows smashed, images and tombs were destroyed or defaced, carved woodwork and books were burnt and vestments shredded. In fact, anything which was considered to have any popish symbolism was destroyed. Parliamentary troops rampaged through many churches and their bullet holes can be seen to this day in some churches e.g. Saint Dyfrog, Llanrhaeadr. We also know that Cromwell's men used to stable their horses in a number of churches. Many of our churches still bear evidence of the iconoclasm which swept through the country.

In February 1646, Parliamentarians used the church at Llansilyn, Montgomeryshire, as a garrison and the doors of this church also bear testimony of their presence. Here they took the opportunity of destroying any images which had previously escaped destruction. They also destroyed the stained glass window which one Ieuan Bach of Henblas and his wife had given to the church in the sixteenth century.

Anglican clergy who had supported the Royalists during the Civil War were removed from their benefices and replaced with Puritan clergy. The churches were to suffer further desecration as a result of various Acts and Orders. Early in the Civil War, Parliament abolished Episcopal government in the Church of England. All church property other than parochial endowments were confiscated, ornaments were removed, and even the Common Prayer Book was declared illegal and its use banned. The royal arms were to be removed and the communion table moved from the chancel into the nave and the Communion became an act of commemoration and far removed from the medieval sacrament of the Mass.

Only churches in the most remote locations could escape such large-scale destruction at the hands of the iconoclasts. As many of the churches in rural Wales would be in this category, we can enjoy today many of the treasures which would otherwise have been lost.

An Act of 1647 required that everyone should swear an oath renouncing the papacy and those who refused to swear were presented to Quarter Sessions.

The Anglican church became established with the restoration of the monarchy in 1660. A new edition of the Book of Common Prayer was published in 1662 with certain changes, and the communion table was restored to its position at the east end of the chancel. The royal arms were also erected in all churches, sometimes with the addition of the words 'My son, fear God and the King, and meddle not with them that are given to change', a timely reminder that there should not be another uprising against the established church.

Twenty years of unrest had left its indelible mark upon the Church.

(iii) 1700–1800

It was the Industrial Revolution that was responsible for the transformation of British society during the second half of the eighteenth century and the first half of the nineteenth century. The big industrial works claimed workers from the land with the resulting increase in urban population. Industry required more and more machinery, which in turn called for better roads and ease of communication. Britain became a powerful industrial nation, but despite this, social and economic problems were to have a considerable effect upon the population for a long time.

The Church's response to such fundamental transformation was, surprisingly, one of complacency. It remained subservient to the government and failed to appreciate the needs of the people during a period of such radical changes. Bishops were political appointments and as such were expected to devote their time to their duties in the House of Lords. This meant that many of them would be absent from their diocese for long periods of time and completely out of touch with their parishioners and their problems. A number of clergy held two or more benefices simultaneously, and had been appointed by lay patrons and enjoyed a very comfortable lifestyle in return for minimal duties, whilst their curates undertook most of the work for a mere pittance. The splendid Georgian rectories are evident of this. To a certain extent, the Church was reluctant to respond to any religious enthusiasm in case it should be regarded as popish sympathy, and was quite satisfied to maintain the status quo. However, such an attitude could not react to the needs of the people, nor did it resolve the very real problems of the disadvantaged. In a number of churches, what seemed important was to uphold the existing social system, at the same time ignoring the religious needs of the community. The Church merely became guardians of the established order.

Unfortunately, the Established Church lost its influence in those areas where there was an explosion of population as a result of the Industrial Revolution, and this created an opportunity for the Nonconformists to establish themselves. Despite this, the Church still touched the lives of the people in a number of ways. It was considered important to be baptized in church even for those who did not regularly attend church, and they got married in church and were buried by the parish priest although they were Nonconformists.

By the nineteenth century the Church had progressed from the medieval church with its mystery and overt superstition. More emphasis was placed on the sermon, and large pulpits of two or three levels were erected in small parish churches as well as in the large parish churches. Galleries were also erected to cater for large congregations.

Parish vestry books give an interesting insight into some of the difficulties relating to church seating. The vestry book for the parish of Eglwys Bach in the Conwy valley gives this account:

> At the Vestry held in the Parish Church at Eglwys Bach on Monday the 11th day of February 1793, the parishioners then and there assembled, it was ordered that whereas Sir Watkin Williams Wynn, Bart's seat encroached too far into the sitting place of Lewis Lloyd Williams of Hafodwyryd, Esq., if the said Lewis Williams will make a decent seat in the church, he shall be allowed one yard in breadth from aisle to aisle to fix the same, and whereas the said Sir Watkin had a greater quantity of ground for sitting places in the old church than appears he has in the new church. It was then ordered that he should have the Bench as sitting place on the south side of his own seat, and one of the five guineas seats on the north side of the church, which will together make for the deficiency.

At a previous Vestry held on 3 December 1792 it was resolved:

> That a certain seat or sitting place on the north side of the altar in the said Parish Church (Eglwys Fach) was to be set up for sale, accordingly the same was sold to John Roberts, representative of John Forbes, Esq., for the sum of £16.7s.6d. And at the same time nos. 41 and 42 in the rage of the seven guineas seats were sold unto Mr Hugh Kyffin, a representative to Sir W. W. Wynne, for the sum of £14.14s.0d. And also no. 14 in the range of the £5.5s.0d. Seats was sold to David Morris representative of Mr Thomas Parry of Ty Gwyn.

There is no doubt that the occupation of certain seats was a matter of great importance so as to uphold social standing.

In time, the class differences caused discontent amongst the congregations and also led to the growth of Nonconformity as an escape from such blatant class distinction. Churchwardens also tried to obtain more power and more income from the box pews and strove to increase the number of such pews, and the wealthier families demanded the best pews commensurate with their wealth and social standing.

However, the Church's apathy in the eighteenth century meant that a large number of churches were allowed to fall into disrepair. This is borne out in the literature of travellers through Wales between 1750 and 1850.

Also, Wales had been a poor country prior to the Reformation and that meant that it was impossible for the churches to be generously endowed. The financial requirement for a man to become a Justice of the Peace was that he should be the owner of land worth £20 per annum, but this figure had to be reduced to £10 per annum in Wales. Indeed, one historian has stated that very few men in north Wales could even attain this reduced figure.

A large number of travellers who came to Wales during this period published accounts of their tours. It is interesting to note that their remarks upon St David's Cathedral are no better than their remarks upon the smallest of parish churches. In 1794, Henry Penruddock Wyndham made a tour of Wales. On his visit to St David's Cathedral his initial surprise was that a cathedral had been built in such a remote area. When he saw the graves inside the cathedral with dead flowers on mounds of earth he criticized the officers of the church for such neglect. Wyndham was not alone in his criticism, and very few had any complimentary remarks to make.

The Revd William Bingley spent three months in north Wales in 1798 and was in the Llanberis area for a time searching for rare alpine plants. He was very disappointed when he saw the church of St Peris, and he wrote:

> The church of Llanberis [Nant Peris today], was, four years ago, without exception, the most ill-looking place of worship I ever beheld. The first time I came to the village, I absolutely mistook it for a large antique cottage, for even the bell tower was so overgrown with ivy as to bear much the appearance of a weather-beaten chimney, and the grass in the churchyard was so long as to hide the few graves stones therein from view.

His description of the house of the curate, the Revd John Morgan, is very similar. It had only two small rooms, and John Morgan wore a long, threadbare blue coat and a blue handkerchief on his head. Bingley saw this as further indication of the impoverished condition of the church as well as the curate. The Revd Peter Bayley Williams, rector of the parish, with whom Bingley stayed, was often unable to hold services in the church because rain was pouring through the roof.

Another traveller with very forthright views was Dr Samuel Johnson. He was in north Wales in the same year as Wyndham. He visited the churches at Tudweiliog and Llangwnnadl in Llŷn in the company of Mrs Thrale and her husband. Mrs Thrale was anxious to visit Plas Bodfel, the house where she was born in January 1740–41, and she was also the proprietor of the tithes of both churches. This is what Dr Johnson had to say about the churches:

> We surveyed the churches, which were mean and neglected to a degree scarcely imaginable. They have no pavements, and the earth is full of holes. One of them has a breach in the roof. On the desk, I think of each lay a folio Welsh Bible of the Black letter, which the curate cannot easily read.

Dr Johnson had encountered in Llŷn what was happening in churches throughout Wales – churches in disrepair, tithes in the hands of laymen and the poor education of the priest. This led to the material and spiritual impoverishment of the churches.

The following interesting comment appeared in the Annual Register for 1788:

> Among the several returns which were read to the House of Commons in compliance with Mr Gilbert's Act, was one from a poor Welsh curate, who, after delineating the

distress of his poor neighbours adds – 'but their distress cannot be greater than mine are. I have a wife who is far advanced in her pregnancy. I have around me nine poor children, for whom I have never yet could procure shoe or stocking. It is with difficulty I can provide them with food. My income is £35 per annum, and for this I do the duty of four parishes'.

Throughout the eighteenth and nineteenth centuries, the churches of Wales were allowed to fall into disrepair either by indifference or lack of appropriate technical knowledge, and their treasures neglected. It would appear that all that was done was to carry out the minimal amount of repair and maintenance. This was a short-term answer to a problem that was left for future generations to resolve.

Robert Roberts, known as *y Sgolor Mawr* (the great scholar), experienced example of this when he was travelling through Anglesey. Just after he had left Llannerch-y-medd he saw a small church by the side of the road. When he went in, what he saw was that:

> The oak seats were slowly rotting to pieces, the font was dismantled and had only a broken pedestal remaining. The altar had no covering of any sort to hide the nakedness of the moth-eaten wood, the rails were awry and loose. I thought at first that the church was entirely abandoned to the bats but the sight of a damp, dingy, ragged surplice hanging over the reading desk, showed that some attempt at a service was still made.

After a period of nearly three centuries of harmful indifference, Church authorities realised that some urgent remedial work was required. They recognized that their attitude towards church buildings was alienating their parishioners, and saw that the number of independent chapels being built was a further problem to them. It was their hope that improved buildings would encourage people to return to the fold and that the importance of the Established Church could be impressed upon them. To many people, the churches had been allowed to deteriorate to such a state that they were often referred to as 'the chief barn of the locality'. In 1846, one report stated:

> We have seen churches so damp and dirty than no gentleman would allow his kitchen to be kept in the same state, the earthen floor worn into pairs of deep holes by the feet of the rustic occupiers of seats during successive generations, the communion table, small and rickety, covered, or rather uncovered by a moth-eaten mouldy cloth, the population of the parish five hundred, the congregation fifty, hard by the church the rectory, a spacious, comfortable and well furnished dwelling, and not many furlongs off, a large and ugly meeting-house with its double range of windows and low pitched roof, well floored, well glazed, well lighted, well warmed, well cleaned and not only well frequented, but inside full galleries and all. And the people thronging the doorways and that not only on Sundays alone but on other days also.

Another traveller in 1803 also expressed concern when he met a number of 'Nonconformists who were so fanatical over their beliefs and with their unbridled zeal in spreading their message'. He was also of the opinion that the Church had fallen into a helpless state and that it was time for it to become aware of the very grave situation which faced it, if it was to survive.

There followed a period when churches were demolished unnecessarily, on the pretence of building a more appropriate structure. New churches were erected in a number of places in Wales which were completely lacking in character, and without regard to the architectural treasures which were being lost at the same time. Churches were also 'improved', and in that process their main architectural features were lost forever. It was clear that positive steps were necessary to restore the authority and influence of the Church if it was to win back its members.

Consequently, a new attitude towards church architecture followed, and with it the desire to return to Gothic style and principles. There was also a generation of wealthy clerics who appreciated the needs of the period and who also possessed the necessary knowledge, and were quite able to undertake the work themselves, One of these new breeds was the Revd John Parker, the Rector of Llanyblodwel and Llanmerewig, near Newtown, Montgomeryshire. He travelled through Wales before many of the churches had been ruined by unsympathetic repairs, and he kept a very detailed description of them, together with outstandingly detailed drawings of their screens and other fittings. Parker maintained that Gothic architecture was the only appropriate style for churches. His detailed work in recording the churches has ensured that the work of those medieval craftsmen was safeguarded and can be better understood today. His manuscript notes in the National Library of Wales at Aberystwyth give a clear indication of his own personal standpoint, which became better understood as the nineteenth century progressed. He wrote:

> The art of Gothic is superior both in practice and design. I doubt not, but that the inventors of it, whosoever they were, entertained a latent hatred of Rome, her style, her system, and above all the mode of building. An architectural secret was discovered that shook the pre-eminence of Rome in this art. The discovery was combined with an expression of solemn and earnest feeling such as the Scriptures could only supply. The inventor of Gothic was to art what the Reformation was to the Christian Religion.

Chapter 5

Church architecture

Immediately following the Reformation, there came a need to improve church buildings to meet the requirements of the new religion, but how was this to be achieved? There were marked differences between the Roman Catholics and the Protestants, and it was necessary to demonstrate these differences. Gothic architecture was considered the best way to meet those demands. Simple wooden tables were erected in the centre of the chancel and replaced the stone altars, because the communion was not to be considered as a recreation of Christ's sacrifice but rather what the sacrifice really meant. The sermon became an important feature of the service and so the pulpit, with its high sound-board, was located in the nave and seats arranged around it.

Gothic Architecture

In turn, Germany, France and England have claimed the discovery of Gothic Architecture. Despite any claims made by England, however, it must be acknowledged that the magnificent choir of Cologne cathedral was in existence when Gothic architecture in Britain was only beginning to supplant Norman architecture, but it developed very quickly in Britain so that it could be compared favourably with the best to be found anywhere. The main features of the new Gothic were clustered columns, and windows separated with columns and fretwork, and this developed its own artistic force. Very soon, however, an excess of ornamentation was to lead to a deterioration of decoration. Some people saw this as reverting once again to the Roman Catholicism they had fought so hard to eliminate. This short-lived glory was to cause delay in the acceptance of Gothic architecture being adopted as the most suitable style for church architecture.

St Bernard and the Cistercians believed that too much ornamentation in churches offended God.

Although an excess of ornamentation was for a time considered ostentatious, it did, however, allow an opportunity to make a detailed study of the possibilities it had to offer, and from such a study, there developed a style which would bring untold benefit and beauty to both large and small churches. An important element of Gothic architecture was the constant search for order and perfection.

Some aspects of the style had already appeared in the Norman period, and elements had been adopted by William the Conqueror in the 1070s and then adopted by the French, but a century was to elapse before it became popular in Britain when the new era of church building began in the 1170s.

The term 'Gothic Architecture' is a loose term used generally for the type that developed from the Romanesque style during the latter half of the twelfth century and which became popular in Europe (but not in Italy) by the middle of the thirteenth century. The aim was to build simple but beautiful churches with ribbed vaults, nave, clerestory windows and side aisles and with large areas for stained glass. Decorative details were primarily developed with the aim of finding the loveliest and most appropriate ornament for churches and it was soon to spread to domestic buildings as well.

Neither the builder/architect of the medieval period, nor their patrons, considered suitability, but rather an excess of competition. When consideration is given to cathedrals across the country it will be clear that economy was not always an over-riding consideration.

Since Gothic architecture was never bound by church canons, which in the past had fixed classical details, it became a style which offered continuous growth and freedom, and it also called for better craftsmanship than the Romanesque. It has always been associated with churches because of the feeling of devotion that was engendered by their size, height and their stained glass windows. The freedom it offered proved to have far-reaching effects since it provided an answer to any architectural problem and also gave an opportunity for new ideas to be developed. By 1725–1750 the style can be seen to have had a great effect on all churches.

Historically, Gothic architecture called for very fine wood carving. This can be seen in a number of rood screens, e.g. Llananno in Radnorshire, Llanwnog in Montgomeryshire and Llanegryn in Merionethshire to name but a few. This craftsmanship called for woodcarvers and stonemasons to be artistic as well as carvers.

Early English Gothic is seen as fresh in style, with carved leaves and flowers, and these became popular on columns, corbels and screens of the period. This was to give birth to still further development and architectural freedom. The geometrical complexity of patterns, however, was considered excessive, and the number of styles clashed with each other. But it still maintained its liveliness to the end of the fifteenth century and on to the sixteenth century, and outside Italy, it had a great influence on the Renaissance architecture which gradually followed it.

The Cambridge and Oxford Societies were supporting studies of church architecture in the 1830s and 1840s. If the Ecclesiologists had been responsible for maintaining a national awareness at the beginning of the nineteenth century, the high churchmen and Puseyites came to play an important part in the second half of the century, particularly after the publication of *The Ecclesiologist*. The Ecclesiologists were concerned that private homes were kept neat and tidy, whilst the House of God was to be found with leaking roofs, damp walls and broken windows. The Protestants, on the other hand, looked upon their recommendations with some scepticism.

From its beginning, the Oxford Movement warned against too many alterations, but despite this, a number of churches were being repaired without any regard to their medieval treasures.

There is no doubt that both the Cambridge and Oxford Societies had a profound influence upon Gothic architecture. When their graduates left the universities they were anxious to revive the nation from its lethargy. A. W. A. Pugin (1812–1852) wanted this to be done by reviving Catholicism, but the Ecclesiologists advocated Gothic architecture as the way forward.

The Evangelists did not consider ceremonies and sacred images to be appropriate. They considered that the chancel, with its rood screen, belonged to the Dark Ages. The altar was a stumbling block to the Protestants and the cross itself was not considered important. Evangelists looked upon the Ecclesiologist and Gothic revival as a threat to Protestantism and the needs of society, and could possibly lead people back to Catholicism. Simplicity in all matters was their aim, and without any suggestion of superstition.

For their part, the Ecclesiologists argued that the Evangelists had allowed the churches to fall into disrepair and that the ceremonies were uninspiring. Children were growing up not understanding church liturgy and the sacraments. Ceremonies at the altars had almost ceased and the chancel had lost its importance and was sometimes used as a vestry. Baptism was often regarded purely as a naming ceremony and frequently performed in the homes rather than in church.

Whilst the revival of Gothic architecture was tied up with the revival of Christianity and although at first associated with Tractarianism and Roman Catholicism, it became to be accepted by the Evangelists.

It was inevitable that such far-reaching changes would have a profound effect upon builders as well as architects. Encaustic tiles were required, together with stained glass windows and quality metalwork, rich materials for vestments, and everything else that was associated with the new style. Architects, artists and craftsmen had to learn the Gothic requirement, with all its attention to details and mouldings. As architectural designs became free from the old classical style, architects found themselves free to experiment.

The influence of the Ecclesiologists coincided with a period of great activity in church building in England, and it was estimated that around a hundred new churches were being built every year from 1840 to the end of the century. It was soon realised, however, that this level of activity could not be sustained and many of the new churches found that they could not maintain themselves.

Ecclesiology

In 1833, the supreme jurisdiction in ecclesiastical matters was transferred to the Judicial Committee of the Privy Council much to the concern of church leaders. Also in 1833 two very influential societies were formed in Oxford and Cambridge Universities – the Oxford Society for the Study of Gothic Architecture, and the Cambridge Society for the Study of Church Architecture, otherwise known as The Camden Society. The Camden Society set out to improve church architecture by visiting churches, making brass rubbings and publishing articles, reviews and photographs. From its inception, this was more than an historical society; it supported medieval craftsmanship as a means of repairing churches and the erection of new churches which would meet liturgical requirements. In 1841 it published *The Ecclesiologist* for the first time and it was one of the most important architectural journals of the period and its influence was felt long after the last issue came from the press in 1868. In essence, Ecclesiology is the study of the organisation and development of the Church and of ecclesiastical architecture and decoration, especially with regard to its liturgical significance, and in this respect, the Society played a most significant role.

It was inevitable that some clergy were suspicious of this new Society and they feared that once again that it advocated a return to Catholicism. They were similarly dubious of the Oxford Movement which had been set up by Keble and Newman. In 1843 the Bishop of Manchester visited one church that had been planned along the lines of these new societies and according to one report following his visit:

He gave an exhibition of manical fury. He cast down

cushions and altar cloths, and he screwed off ornaments and dashed them on the pavement, and expressed a wish, that the boys might break the stained glass windows in the church.

Gradually, a number of young clerics and some bishops came to appreciate the Camden Society with its enthusiasm for the new spirit of the age. The architect A. C. Pugin prepared a practical handbook on Gothic architecture. On his death, the work was carried on by his son, Augustus Welby Pugin, who subsequently became a Roman Catholic. He was a passionate believer in Gothic architecture as being the only style suitable for churches. His book *An Apology for the Revival of Christian Architecture* was influential in establishing Gothic architecture once and for all, and by 1845 it had become successful everywhere.

In 1845, the Camden Society ceased and its name was changed to the Ecclesiological Society. It broke its connection with Cambridge and became a national society with its headquarters in London.

Although eighteenth-century builders had removed a number of rood screens and rearranged the seating and the pulpit, efforts were made to undo their work, because, after all, not everyone could accept Gothic architecture, John Nash (who was responsible for restoration work at St David's cathedral before George Gilbert Scott later undid his work) said, 'I hate this Gothic style. One window costs more trouble in designing than two houses ought to'. When some architects adopted the Gothic style they were often selective and arbitrary and ignored historical accuracy.

George Gilbert Scott was responsible for the restoration of

the cathedrals at St David's in 1864, Bangor in 1866 and St Asaph in 1869. He had very strong opinions on the restoration of old churches, and in his book *Personal and Professional Recollections*, published in 1870, he wrote:

> The country has been, and continues to be, actually devastated with destruction under the name of restorers. For years and years the vast majority have been committed to men who neither know nor care anything whatever about them, and out of whose hands they have emerged in a condition truly deplorable, stripped of almost everything which gave them interest and value.

Gothic Architecture in England

Although the pointed arch occurs spasmodically in England in various buildings dating from the second half of the twelfth century, English Gothic first appears in its final form in the choir of Canterbury Cathedral, built by the French architect William of Sens.

There were two main differences between English and French work. The first was that in England there was no rivalry between the regular and secular clergy, as there had been in France. The monasteries had been powerful everywhere, and the influence of the Cistercian Order, with its insistence on simplicity and restraint, was very important as, in no small part, was the English adoption of the square east end rather than the apse, as well as the development of the moulded capital without foliage, together with varied moulding profiles. The tradition of Norman church building strengthened the English Gothic love of simple wall finishing, in contrast with the French. No attempts were made in England to follow the soaring heights of

French churches, nor the lavish use of carved ornament and sculpture.

Early English Gothic (1180–1275)
This was the time when a new, complete plan for the English church was adopted after the Norman period, with pointed lancet windows being so characteristic of the period. Decoration was minimal and consisted mainly of finely-carved but formal stiff-leaf foliation, mainly found on capitals and in windows and doorway mouldings, together with dogtooth ornaments and crockets. The Early English practice of grouping two or more lancet windows beneath a single arch created the tracery-ornamental stone mouldings within a window.

The Decorated Period (1275–1375)
By the middle of the thirteenth century the use of rich tracery had become common, and the decorative lavishness that was seen everywhere gave rise to the second period of English Gothic, and became known as the Decorated Period. The second half of the century was known as Geometric because of the development of bar tracery. Decoration also became more elaborate in the form of stone carving and stained glass. Carved ornaments became increasingly vigorous and natural, evolving into more stylised forms, and the four-leaved flower or ballflower ornament is a good example of this. Exceptional carving of this period is to be found on the western façade of Wells Cathedral. Despite this, however, it was considered that it did not allow sufficient scope for the imagination, and the beginning of the fourteenth century saw the evolvement of

curvilinear tracery producing flame-like shapes, and subsequently reticulated tracery with circles forming a lattice of ogee shapes. Elegant columns and corbels and the triforium were combined to express an air of mystery and richness that was to be found only in churches.

All this was followed by a considerable improvement in church furniture such as the pulpit and especially the screens, and it was here that wood carving was seen at its best, when all sorts of leaves, symbols and heraldry combined to make outstanding works of art.

Perpendicular Style (1375–1545)

English medieval architecture reached its climax with the Perpendicular style of the late fourteenth and fifteenth centuries. This was also the period which saw great activity in refurbishing and extending churches. The Perpendicular style was characterized by the delicate vertical tracery of the widows and stone panelling, together with fluted piers leading upwards into intricate fan-shaped vaulting. Whilst cathedrals and large churches offered greater opportunities for this style, smaller country churches could also adapt certain features for their windows and pulpits. These elements are just as important to be kept for future generations as any other treasures to be found in the churches. It is only by retaining such features that we can appreciate the bigger picture, and see how everything was working towards perfection.

Perhaps it was not necessary to have completely new churches immediately after the Reformation, but as they fell into disrepair, and their congregation increased, it then became necessary for new churches to be erected, reflecting the new emphasis from the altar to the pulpit; and this can be seen in the smaller churches too. This was the period for the Gothic style to demonstrate its true splendour.

Despite the fact that the Cistercian order was the most popular in Wales, with its magnificent buildings still to be seen around the country, it did not have any influence on church architecture as such, nor on the Gothic style, although the style was found in their monasteries. The order may have been close to the people but it did nothing to promote craftsmanship as the handmaiden of their religion. Cistercian life was one of simple communal living and austerity, and their churches were devoid of ornament. Their Rule prohibited stone belfries, and the only statue allowed was one of Christ. All monks wore habits of undyed wool (hence they became known as 'white monks'). Precious stones were not to be used in communion vessels.

Whilst the order did not have considerable impact on church architecture, it was not until the fifteenth century that anxieties about fine art were finally laid to rest, but by this time the order had lost its influence.

The Gothic Revival

In the eighteenth century, when cultural refinements were at a low ebb, there were those who called for the return of some elements of Gothic architecture, and its revival is reflected in our churches.

Gothic Revival began in earnest with the rebuilding of the Palace of Westminster in 1834, when the architects Sir Charles Barry and Augustus Pugin created a neo-Gothic masterpiece containing ornamentation and craftsmanship of the highest order. At the time, there was a reaction against what the Victorians, in particular, perceived to be eighteenth-century vulgarity, both architectural and liturgically. The classical style was seen as 'pagan' and decadent, and the Gothic style was perceived as ridiculous. In its place came a return to the 'true architecture of Christianity', that of the thirteenth and fourteenth centuries.

The Gothic Revival was not simply an architectural movement but was inspired by idealists such as John Ruskin (1819–1900), who believed that only those who lived a good and moral life could creat anything that was truly worthwhile. They abhorred anything artificial. The best guidelines for Gothic designs had been set out in *The Ecclesiologist*. Sir Gilbert Scott (1811–1878) became its leading exponent between 1855 and 1885, when church building was once again to the fore.

An inspection of church architecture today will reveal that not only did Gothic style survive, but also that it was the best expression of a style we have ever had. It is an important reminder of the time before the Industrial Revolution.

Norman door, Strata Florida c. 1175

Early English, 1260

Decorated, 1320

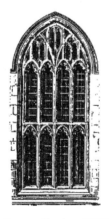

Perpendicular, 1386

Chapter 6

The Oxford Movement

Many movements have had an impact upon the Anglican church over the centuries, affecting both its architecture and its liturgy. One such was the Oxford Movement of the nineteenth century, with its aim of restoring high church principles at a time of increasing theological liberalism. Many ceremonies and sacraments had disappeared after the Reformation and the Movement wanted to restore dignity to the services. They also advocated two daily services – the reading of morning and evening prayers – and aimed to perform the Sacrament every week.

The 1830s were very distressing years for many churchmen and they could not have anticipated how helpless the church would be when faced with a state that was determined to reform it, and to redistribute its property. They could not accept a situation whereby the Church was to be reformed by an outside authority, whilst they insisted that the Church's authority was derived from the fact that its bishops were of apostolic succession.

The Church had become very unpopular at the time of the Reform Bill of 1832, and some thought that it was inevitable that it would soon be disestablished. Bishops, deans and prebendaries, as well as the country parson, were represented in cartoons as fat and worldly. Dr Arnold, the headmaster of Rugby School, thought that no human could save the Church as it then stood. The danger, however, was averted by the reform of the tithe system and the re-arrangement of the dioceses, and plurality and non-residence were abolished. Despite the fact that some attempts at reform were made, some high churchmen were still not satisfied.

The Oxford Movement was sparked off in July 1833 when John Keble (1792–1866) preached a sermon at the University church at Oxford criticising a Bill for the suppression of ten Irish bishops. Between 1833 and 1841, Keble, Edward Pusey (1800–1882) and John Newman (1801–1890) issued a series of pamphlets (*Tracts of the Times*) stating their position, and urging a comprehensive study of theology, ecclesiastical history, liturgy and evangelism. They believed that the Church of England was threatened by secular power and that the Reform Act of 1832 would strengthen the position of 'liberals and dissenters'. They sought to defend the Anglican church as a divine institution and assert its authority. Their cardinal doctrine was that the Church of England was part of the visible Holy Catholic church and had an unbroken connection with the primitive church, and impressed the importance of the Sacraments. They also wanted the Book of Common Prayer to be the Rule of their faith.

Members of the Movement became known as Tractarians, and they strongly emphasized the importance of the ministry and ceremonial of the Church, and by so doing, demonstrated the continuity of the Catholic faith.

Although it gained influential support, the Bishops attacked the Movement, and there were a number of conversions to the Roman Catholic church, including John Newman in 1841, who subsequently became a Cardinal in 1879. With Newman's withdrawal, the leadership of the Oxford Movement fell to

Pusey, the main champion of the high church movement, who advocated union with the Roman Catholic church. Newman maintained that without his leadership the Movement would have foundered in its early years.

As the Movement's aim was to protect the church from the involvement of secular government, it was inevitable that it would raise many arguments both for and against its aim. Many politicians and churchmen were opposed to their ideas because they sought to elevate the Church above the State and re-establish the Church of England with full Catholic doctrine and ritual. Welsh periodicals of the period give clear indication of the strength of feeling. It wasn't prudent for the Puseyites (as they became known) to declare themselves as Catholics as this would have meant the end of the Movement before it had the opportunity to become established. There was strong opposition to it because some considered it too high church, and some went so far as to say that its leaders were secret agents for the Pope.

The Movement came into being at a time when great concern was expressed at the structural state of church buildings and ceremonies. Also, there was a need for the Church to reassert its authority in the country and stem the rush of its members towards Nonconformity. The Church had become very unpopular and the nonconformists were able to benefit from this. Robert Roberts gives a vivid account of the position in north Wales in his autobiography, together with the influence that the Movement exerted in the area. He attributes the problems to Anglicanisation and nepotism, which had been hostile to its growth and popularity for generations.

As the Movement grew, emphasis was placed on the rituals

and ceremonies which had been lost since the Reformation. This led to the priest wearing a white surplice instead of black, and to the priest facing the altar during communion, thus turning his back on the congregation.

The Movement also had an influence upon church architecture and sculpture. Gothic architecture and decorations became important in new churches, although the Gothic revival had preceded the Movement with the restoration of churches at the beginning on the nineteenth century. High churchmen did not favour the classical traditions of the eighteenth century or those churches which gave an outward appearance of being a Nonconformist chapel. This also supported the Gothic Revival and set out firm foundations for others to follow.

One Welshman was to play an important part in the formation of the Movement, namely Isaac Williams, who was the son of a wealthy barrister in London but was born at Cwmcynfelin near Aberystwyth. He was educated at Harrow and Trinity College, Oxford, where he graduated with BA and MA and became a Fellow of his college.

At Llangorwen, his family erected the first church specifically to spread the Tractarian Movement's teaching in 1841, and it soon became known as the 'Pusyist church'. In it is to be found a stone altar – one of the very few stone altars erected after the Reformation. It was here that the use of white vestments by the priest was started.

From the day that Llangorwen's church was opened, the practice of morning prayers continued unbroken for a period of twenty years. Here also, all church festivals were kept. Isaac Williams was amongst the first pioneers of church reform in

Wales. Because of his connection with Newman, he was at the centre of the high church movement in the University. He took an active part in publishing *The Tract of the Times*. He was steeped in the established theology of the church, but he was never tempted by the principles and customs of the Roman Catholic church, and he could not accept the papist tendencies of Newman.

At Llangorwen, there is a lectern in the form of an eagle and carved from one piece of oak, which was the gift of John Keble. In the church also, there are six bronze candelabras in the Gothic style, believed to have been the gift of John Newman.

The only bishop in Wales to have shown any support for the Movement from the start was Christopher Bethel, Bishop of Bangor (1830–1859). Into his diocese came a number of young clerics who had come under the influence of the Movement, and who were anxious to spread its principles. Amongst them were Philip Constable Ellis, Morris Williams (whose bardic name was *Nicander*) and Evan Lewis who became Dean of Bangor. But Morris Williams was the pioneer of the Movement in Wales. He was an undergraduate of Jesus College from 1831 to 1836. He served curacies at Holywell, Bangor, and Llanllechid near Bangor, and he spent his remaining years as curate at Amlwch and Llanwenllwyfo. Whilst at Holywell, his mastery of the Welsh language led to him being appointed Secretary of the Prayer Book Commission in 1841. He attracted into the Movement all literary-minded students and younger clergy, and gave it a Welsh identity. It is estimated that one third of the priests in the diocese were supporters of the Movement when Bethel died.

A new church was also built in the parish of Llanllechid,

Caernarfonshire, and Robert Roberts described it as 'in the early Gothic style of architecture, plain but neat, with open seats and other accessories of the revival'.

Many were disappointed with the growth of the Movement and especially with the practice of lighting tall candles on the altar and the placing of a cross on the communion table. They were also concerned that churches were being decorated with paintings and with images of the saints. The superstitious reverence shown to the white vestments of the priests, and all other popish elements, were also frowned upon.

Prior to the Protestant Reformation it was customary to put one, and certainly no more than two, candles on the altar – one at each side of the cross. Over time this custom developed to allow any number of candles, and three at each side of the cross came to be considered more effective. There was a great deal of opposition to this development, and in 1890 the right to place so many candles on the altar was challenged in law. The custom was, however, confirmed.

Chapter 7

The Iconostasis and the rood loft

Early church services were notable for their spirit of intense respect. It was very important that the distinction between the priest and his congregation be maintained in a way which was clear to everyone. For this reason wooden beams hung with drapes were erected to keep the altar from the sight of the congregation. These curtains formed the earliest screens and it became an act of sacrilege for anyone apart from the priest to pass beyond them.

With the passing of the years the screens became extremely important and the cloth was only to be used on special occasions. This development led to more permanent screens being adopted. The curtained screens were incredibly similar to the Jewish Tabernacle referred to in the book of Exodus, Chapter Twenty-six:

31. Make a curtain of blue, purple and scarlet yarn and finely twisted linen, with cherubim worked into it by a skilled craftsman
32. Hang it with gold hooks on four posts of acacia wood overlaid with gold and standing on four silver bases
33. Hang the curtain from the clasps and place the ark of the Testimony behind the curtain. The curtain will separate the Holy Place from the Most Holy Place

The beams which held the cloth screens came to be used to hold candles and effigies – as in the Iconostasis, the name used in eastern churches for the screens that hold effigies or paintings.

The screen created a barrier which prevented a person without authority from passing through it. In Latin the screens were called *cancelli* (which is where the words 'chancel' and '*cangell*' originated from), and as the importance of the screens grew, the craftsmen who made them had the opportunity to display their talents and produce the special fretwork which can be seen in the screens of the Middle Ages.

The Reverend Richard Hooker (1553–1600), a very influential theologian in the age of Elizabeth I, who bore much of the responsibility for the reorganisation and reformation of the Church at that time, placed great importance on keeping the chancel separate. Hooker said;

> Our churches are places provided that the people may there assemble themselves in due and decent manner according to their several degrees and order. Which thing being common unto us with Jews, we have in this respect our churches divided by certain partitions, though not so many in numbers as theirs ... There being in ours for local distinction between the clergy and the rest ... but one partition, the cause whereof at the first (it seemeth) was, that as many as were capable of the Holy Mysteries might there assemble themselves, and no other creep amongst them.

Within half a century of Hooker, one English Bishop was asking churches this question:

> Is your chancel divided from the nave or body of your church with a partition of stone, boards, wainscot, gates

or otherwise? Wherein is there a decent strong door to open or shut (as occasion serveth), with lock and key to keep out boys, girls, or irreverent men and women?

It is believed that the custom of erecting screens in parish churches came into being at the beginning of the fourteenth century, and that prior to this they were to be found only in the larger churches. There were at least two reasons for the use of screens. Firstly, the cult of the saints had become very important and churches needed to put statues or pictures of saints onto panels; in this way the screen was similar to the Iconostasis of the eastern churches. Secondly, the crucifix, which had previously hung in the chancel, could now be placed standing above the screen.

By having a solid screen, it was a small matter to build a loft above it, and that is the beginning of the rood loft.

There were two important reasons for the existence of the rood loft. Firstly, it was used to locate a pulpit for Bible readings, psalm singing and so forth. Singing psalms had become more important over time and the loft was to be used by the singers alone.

The second reason was that it was used as an Iconostasis to hold the crucifix, lamps or candles and occasionally to hold an altar as well. It was also used to hold the cloth that at times covered the Crucifix. On the front they showed pictures or carvings of the saints and apostles along with symbols or coats of arms of the gentry.

As an Iconostasis the loft was condemned during the Protestant Reformation, and because of the superstitious nature of the people it was forbidden to use it to hold the carvings noted above. Despite this, some images were allowed to remain if they had an educational element.

It does not appear that there was any opposition to the loft being used as a pulpit, but this use came to an end when pulpits came to be built in the body of the church. The lofts were used by the singers long after the Protestant Reformation.

The giant step that Henry VIII took in abolishing the monasteries led in turn to the Protestant Reformation, and the destruction of a number of churches. As a result, a great deal of the carved woodwork from the monasteries was scattered to the four corners of the earth, but only some of it to the churches. Although evidence of this is scarce, there is room to believe that the screen in Montgomery church came from Churbury abbey.

The year 1547 was a year of great importance for the parish churches, because before this very little change had occurred within them. Putting candles in front of effigies was banned in 1538 when it was decreed that 'onely that light that might commonly goeth about the crosse of the church by the roodloft, the light before the Sacrament of the Altar, and the light above the sepulchure' was allowed. In 1547 it was decreed that every candle was to be banned except the two on the altar, and this 'for the signification "that Christ is the very true Light of the World" they shall suffer to remain'. At the same time every idol which had been misused by the pilgrims, and anything that had had a miracle attributed to it, was to be destroyed. Shortly after this, another decree came banning all idols without exception.

The destruction of the idols during the reign of Edward VI had possibly been responsible for the defacement of the lofts' facades, but the lofts themselves had not been condemned as such. In some churches the Ten Commandments, the Lord's Prayer, the Creed and the Beatitudes were painted instead of the decorations.

The last years of Edward VI saw great damage to the churches as idols, frescos and altars, as well as the reredos, were destroyed.

This destruction of the beauty of the churches was of great concern to the people who still identified with them. In our days of freedom when our rights and our homes are almost sacred, and every kind of artwork is within the reach of everyone, it is hard to grasp how much the churches, with their holy symbols and carvings, meant to the people. Because their houses were so poor and so lacking in decoration the churches offered a haven from day-to-day problems, where the people could shelter and receive salvation.

When Mary came to the throne in 1553 an effort was made to restore the churches to the state they had been in before 1547, and new statues were erected to take the place of those ruined. Pugin said:

> Everything was done to remove the objectionable things that had been introduced during Edward's reign. The text of Scripture that had been placed on the screen and walls were washed out, and in one instance, the cloth painted with the Commandments which had hung before the screen was taken down and cut into surplices.

It is important to pay close attention to the terms used in the orders regarding rood lofts. The orders were definitely not to pull the lofts down but rather to 'alter', 'reform', 'transport' or 'translate' them. This suggests that there was no opposition to the lofts as such but rather that it was the tabernacle-style work which was considered unacceptable. It was this that allowed their continued use by musicians and their instruments.

Although the rood loft was the main glory of the church, this glory was destroyed in the era of Elizabeth I, and it is highly possible that those that did not contain statues or paintings of the saints survived only because they were of no interest to the iconoclastic zeal of the 'reformers'. It is certain too that the fretwork and decorations that did remain were of a type that did not offend the Puritans.

Cromwell's time, in its turn, was responsible for the destruction of yet more lofts. However, there can be no doubt that it was the 'restorers' of the nineteenth century who caused the most damage. In addition, a group of Evangelistic clerics, who neither liked nor understood the screens, came to power. They preferred totally open churches, free from obstacles, which allowed priests and congregations to worship without any sense of the old divisions that these clerics considered not only unnecessary, but also obstacles to worship. It was important to them that the priest could be seen and heard by the whole congregation.

At the beginning of the eighteenth century there was a tendency within the Church to adopt new arrangements. The old traditions were weakening and new ideas were coming to the forefront which sometimes ignored the old principles almost completely. At the same time a period of apathy settled upon church matters.

Although the century had produced significant developments, very little consideration had been given to the traditional turning points in church history. Evangelical zeal was forging ahead, but the old traditions, which had existed since the early days, had almost come to be considered Papist elements.

By the end of the eighteenth century the custom of building a loft for the singers on the western side of the church was generally accepted, and this again was one of the factors responsible for the final disappearance of the rood loft.

The best example in Wales of a loft very similar to the Iconostasis is the one in Llananno church, Radnorshire, with its twenty-five effigies of the Old Testament prophets, the saints and the apostles. It is interesting to note how similar this screen and loft are to the Iconostasis which can be seen in the Kewrfon church in Brittany – which also has fifteen effigies of the saints.

Chapter 8

Chancel Screens I

In the eighteenth and nineteenth centuries it became fashionable, if not a craze, to remove and destroy the rood lofts of the middle ages. Fortunately, the result was not as great in some counties as it was in others. In Anglesey, the result was devastating, for only one screen has survived and that is the one in Llaneilian church near Amlwch, and this is a truly fine screen. The screen would have been the main feature in the medieval churches of Wales. Although they were in existence in the fourteenth century, those which have survived are mainly of the fifteenth and sixteenth centuries. The fact that they have survived so long makes them worthy of the greatest care that we can provide.

Sir Samuel Rush Meyrick (1783–1848), the author of the *History and Antiquities of the County of Cardigan*, which was published in 1809, wrote that at that time only eight screens remained in the county: i.e. at Lampeter, Ystrad, Llangeitho, Ysbyty Ystwyth, Llanddeiniol, Llanilar, Llanwnnen and Llanbadarn Fawr. The following was what he noted about the screen at Llanbadarn Fawr:

> The chancel and north transept are separated from the rest of the church by a light and elegant carved screen, which from the elaborate workmanship they display, were probably erected about the time of Henry VII. It is coloured red, green and yellow, and although once very

brilliant, are now so covered with dirt as to be scarcely perceptible.

In 1868, the church at Llanbadarn Fawr was extensively restored. The plaster and wall paintings were removed; there was, apparently, no need for that to be done, but it was reported that the Vicar at the time had no interest in them. People were calling for the restoration work on such an important and historic church to be placed in the hands of qualified craftsmen, but unfortunately, the appeal fell on deaf ears.

During the restoration work, one visitor wrote as follows:

> When the masons were taking down the old walls of the western part of the church, they noted a variety of colour under the whitewash, this induced them to examine them more closely, when they discovered letters and inscriptions and full length figures in fresco, one being sixteen square yards, including the border, two of which are now partially visible, the other had been entirely destroyed by the workmen before any discovery was made. The principle figure evidently represents St Peter. The full face is partially visible, with the nimbus, and with his right hand extended towards a lioness sitting on her haunches near her den, which is castellated and immediately above the hand is a young ass. There is a key in the hand. The dress was originally scarlet and purple but from the effects of the lime wash the scarlet has become brown and the purple a light blue, it is large and folded, like the Roman toga. There is no inscription under the figure, which is on the wall immediately in front of the south entrance into the church. The other

figure represents a man in chain armour, with a large shield, the profile of the face is indistinct, and to all appearances, with a coronet on his head with a Welsh inscription under it.

There is a peculiarity pertaining to these that is worthy of note, in as much that they represent three distinct periods. First, the original painting is scarlet and purple with a border of twisted columns. This was covered over with white wash on which a fresh painting was laid in yellow with a square border of brown and yellow, and inscriptions with large capital letters in black, this again was white washed and repainted brown with inscriptions. The letters are of good bold characters of the fifteenth century, but time or man has so defaced that beyond the words 'Pardon' and 'Dedd' little can be made out.

The walls and inside jambs of the lancet windows evidently show the action of fire. By a reference to the early history of the church I find that it was burnt down five times in the early wars, viz. in 720 by the Saxons in the reign of Roderick Molwynog, 988 by the Danes in the reign of Meredith ap Owen, 1038 by Llewelyn ap Sisyllt in the reign of Iago ap Idwal, 1071 by the Danes in the reign of Bleddyn ap Cynfryn, 1106 by Ithel ap Madog in the reign of Griffith ap Cynan and in 1111 it was rebuilt, or rather restored by Gilbert Strongbow, Earl of Strygil, and given by him to the monastery of St Peter's, Gloucester.

We may therefore, draw this conclusion that the figure fronting the grand entrance to the church was originally intended to represent St Peter in compliment to the monks of the monastery at Gloucester under whose protection the church had been placed.

The other figure in armour may represent Gilbert Strongbow, Earl of Strygil, particularly as this figure is represented in a coronet and an inscription in Welsh as a compliment, or towards reconciliation with the Welsh people of the district, which it had lately conquered, but, unfortunately the inscription is so defaced it is impossible to make out a sentence.

This splendid and almost perfect fresco painting is now obliterated forever to the great disgrace of the architect and committee of management now superintending the restoration of the old church. Such vandalism is totally unworthy of Cardiganshire.

Another writer at the time reported that parochial taste in the locality was extremely low and that there was no reason why such a building – historically one of the most important in Wales – should not have been rescued from the hands of those who destroyed it.

The frescos at Llanbadarn Fawr had survived the test of time from 1111 to 1869 only to be destroyed forever. The appeal that fell on deaf ears at Llanbadarn Fawr was echoed in many churches throughout Wales.

Only a fraction of past glory now remains and the account of what happened at Llanbadarn Fawr merely underlines the attitude of the Victorian age towards church architecture, frescos and screens.

The late Canon Maurice H. Ridgway BA, FSA, the acknowledged expert on Welsh screens and lofts, wrote an article in 1947 wherein he stated:

> At the time of the Reformation the Principality was a treasure house of church craftsmanship, when however, we consider the upheavals and disturbances which have occurred, religious, social and civic, between 1540 and 1940, it seems wonderful that the devastation of the treasures has not been more complete.

Whilst we may not know the names of the medieval craftsmen who were responsible for creating such treasures, Canon Ridgway refers to centres at Newtown and Montgomeryshire where such work would have been carried out for quite a considerable area, and these craftsmen had an:

> instinctive understanding of the nature of timber, especially in its sinuous strength, and the freedom it attainted from architectural shibboleths, this last was a Welsh quality of mind born of independence of spirit and a disregard for rules and regulations imposed from without.

The use of colours on the screens was also important and this enabled the craftsmen to highlight certain details and simple shadows gave a pleasing effect. This is true craftsmanship which cannot be properly appreciated today since all colours have been removed. Craftsmen of the middle ages did not hesitate to use rich colours and much of the woodwork in the churches would also have been gilded. Unfortunately, no screen exists in Wales today that retains its original colouring, except perhaps, such sections as may have been retained as reredos. Images would also have been painted, and the Welsh bard Sion Cent (fl. 1400–1430) wrote:

A phaentiwr delw a phwyntil,
Yn paentio delwau lawer,
A llu o saint a lliw ser.

(An image painter with a pencil/painted numerous images/and a host of saints in the colour of the stars)

No written description can do justice to these magnificent screens, and Canon Ridgway also wrote:

> If the workmanship was at times rough and ready the effect was nevertheless highly successful, and if at times they became exuberant in the use of surface decoration it was because they delighted in it. They knew that the further away from the eye the work was placed, the simpler, stronger and rougher must be the design and execution, for it to tell in the general scheme.

There can be no doubt that they were skilful craftsmen. By careful study of the screens today it is possible to appreciate the way in which these craftsmen worked by studying their chisel marks and this makes them much more interesting that the machine work of today.

It is a calamity that so much of the works of those craftsmen have been lost to us, especially the screen that was in St Mary's church, Newtown. We must rely on the copious notes of the Revd John Parker and compare them with the screen at Llananno to have some understanding of its beauty.

One cannot but agree with Canon Ridgway that these craftsmen displayed a degree of exuberance in the use of surface decoration in their work, and that it should now remain the mainstay of our heritage. These national treasures must never again be left in the hands of restorers who cannot appreciate their intrinsic beauty and their value. By the end of the nineteenth century, however, this craftsmanship had lost its appeal.

The division of the church with a screen is not unique to western churches nor to the Celtic church. In his book *Liturgy and Ritual of the Celtic Church*, Warren writes:

> The veil, which was such an integral part of the Temple ritual, was no less so in the churches of our ancestors. It continued in full use between the chancel and nave till the end of the twelfth century, and after that was retained until the Reformation from the evening before the first Sunday in Lent till Thursday before Easter, and was called Velum Quadregesimale or Lentern Veil. In the very earliest period it is possible that the veil alone divided the Sanctuary from the nave, but as time went on the division became more solid.
>
> As nothing survived in Britain of the actual construction of our Celtic ancestors, we are dependent upon such information as may be gleaned from early writings on this point. It seems clear from old descriptions that there was a solid screen between nave and chancel having doors in it, these doors being divided by veils and the screen decorated by paintings.

Not all screens were designed to hold a loft with perhaps an organ, singers and their instruments, and consequently many were damaged by excessive weight, but more were destroyed by changes in the liturgy. In the nineteenth century it became fashionable to open the screens to enable the congregation to feel part of the service. Despite opposition in some quarters, very little attention was paid to it.

In reality, the screen is more of a symbolism than anything else – it represents the veil that Christ went through to intercede for us. But it also served as a reminder of the difference between the priest and his congregation and the mystery associated with it.

One authority, however, suggests that too much emphasis has been paced on the division between the chancel and the nave; that the nave was nothing more than the place for the lay folk and used by them for assembly and worship; and that until the advent of high screens in the fourteenth and fifteenth centuries it would have been possible for laymen to witness most of the offices.

There can be no doubt at all that the screens had considerable artistic merit, and despite the fact that a few of them were merely rails in front of the altar. Nothing adds so much to that most potent of all effects in church architecture as a screen, with its vistas half-hidden, half-revealed, of the beautiful and holy things. Wordsworth wrote:

> Keep the charm of not too much,
> Part seen, imagined part.

When oak screens replaced those constructed of stone, they were always in two parts – the bottom part being of solid panels which sometimes contained blind fretwork, and the upper part open with tracery work so that the congregation could view the altar. If a church had a wealthy benefactor, the panels would have been painted with figures of saints. When these are inspected today, it becomes clear that neither time nor cost was too much for the craftsmen who created these works of art, as the magnificently decorated cornice of many screens will illustrate.

It is interesting to note the carvings on some screens and the variety of motifs which can be used as a means of dating them – very often the only means. An excellent example of this can be found on the screen at St Mary's church, Conwy – its history appears to have been recorded in its carvings. It contains the heraldic badge of Sir Richard Pole, Constable of Conwy Castle from 1488 until his death in 1504, in the form of an eagle's claw in red grasping a silver fish. Before coming to Conwy, Pole held a similar appointment at Ludlow, and whilst there he had a close relationship with the young Prince Arthur. The Prince's personal badge of three feathers in the manner which he displayed them, a greyhound and the red dragon of Cadwaladr, are also carved on the screen. Other royal badges found on it are the Tudor rose, portcullis, falcon and fetter lock.

In 1501, Prince Arthur married Catherine of Aragon and her heraldic badge was the pomegranate. The carving on the upper section of the bressumer beam displays the Tudor rose and the lower section shows the pomegranate representing both Arthur and Catherine. These fix the date of the screen to be no earlier than 1498 and not later than 1504.

The poppy heads on each side of the screen opening contain a niche where a small metal or ivory image would have been placed. Similar details are to be found in the church in Ludlow and, as this sort of ornamentation is very rare, it confirms the close connection that Sir Richard Pole had with Ludlow and Conwy castle.

The Conwy screen, however, is not of Welsh design and it is quite possible that it was constructed at Ludlow. Could it be that Sir Richard Pole was responsible for it? Be that as it may, what makes this an outstanding screen is the magnificent example of fan vaulting underneath the floor of the loft. It is difficult to find an example of fan vaulting that would surpass this in richness and completeness. This screen, with its heraldic and other designs, is an exceptional example of sixteenth-century craftsmanship.

However, it is not only in the larger churches that elaborate screens are to be found. A number of small rural churches in Wales also display beautiful screens. In the church at Llananno in Radnorshire is to be found one of the best examples in Wales, and excellent examples are also to be found at Llanwnog, Montgomeryshire and at Llanegryn, Merionethshire and again at Partrishow (*Patrisio*), Radnorshire. Each one of these churches is worthy of a visit. From an architectural point of view none of these churches merit much attention, but certainly the screens which are to be found in them bear testimony to the un-named craftsmen who were responsible for their creation.

We are fortunate in Wales that so many screens have survived; very few of the parishioners would have been familiar enough with the English language in the twenty years following the Reformation to take notice of the orders issued as to what was considered appropriate to remain in the churches. It is also possible that many of the churches were too remote to attract the attention of the Commissioners appointed to ensure that the necessary work of removing the rood loft and images had been carried out.

There are certain characteristic which are peculiar to Welsh screens, such as the open tracery to be found on the eastern side of screens such as at Partrishow and Llanegryn, for example. There is also a wealth of tabernacle work, such as at Llanrwst. A diversity of carvings of animals etc. is also more frequently encountered on Welsh screens than on English screens.

Very little influence of English craftsmanship is to be found in Wales, although this might have been expected in the border counties. A small number of screens constructed in England are to be found in Wales but they did not influence Welsh construction nor their designs. Some screens are to be found where there was a considerable English influence, such as at Conwy, Gresford (*Gresffordd*) or Usk (*Brynbuga*), but Welsh craftsmen completely ignored the work of their English counterpart and kept their individuality. Many of the screens to be found in England, especially in Devon, were influenced by the Renaissance, but it had very little effect in Wales. A number of screens in Cheshire, for example, bear inscriptions, but there are no such examples to be found in Wales.

A small number of screens of Welsh construction are to be found in England such as at St Margret's in Herefordshire. There is a strong similarity between that screen and the one at Llanwnog. There was also a similar screen at Daresbury, Cheshire, at one time.

Welsh craftsmen did not favour the repetition of patterns, as found on English screens, and this will be confirmed by an inspection of the variety of tracery to be found at the top of any screen. On the screen at Llanrwst, for example, you will find carvings of pigs eating acorns, together with symbols of the Passion and vine leaves. Of course, there are examples of magnificent screens to be found in England, but they do tend to be monotonous in their design and following the same pattern again and again. Almost without exception, carvings on English screens will be of birds, and they do not show the same element of freedom and imagination that is found in their Welsh counterpart. The screen at Llananno has been described as 'an effervescence of richness and with a delicate frothy lightness'.

The oak screens are quite different from those that were constructed of stone. The new craftsmen rejected completely the patterns used previously by the stonemasons, and they rejoiced in the new-found freedom the new material offered them. These craftsmen were in an unique position in the development of the screen.

Very few screens were erected immediately following the Reformation, but by the early seventeenth century the Church felt strong enough to embark on re-building churches and screens – but without the rood loft, and certainly without the rood itself, which had been the subject of such condemnation. The rood was an integral part of the screen before the days of Henry VIII. The cross would have been gilded but the instructions to destroy it had been explicit and the work thorough.

When Thomas Dingley wrote *An account of the Progress of His Grace Henry the first Duke of Beaufort through Wales in 1684,* he referred to the church at Llanrwst, and wrote:

> Over the timber arch of the chancel near the Rood loft lieth hid the ancient figure of the Crucifiction as big as the life, this I suppose is shown to none but the curious, rarely even to them.

The space between the rood loft and the roof would, in some instances, be filled in by a tympanum, and a primitive example of this can be found at the church in Llaneleu in Breconshire dating from the fourteenth century, thus maintaining a link with the older Celtic churches. This is an early description of it:

It is closed to the eastern side by a close boarded tympanum diapered with flowers on a coloured ground of distemper, and it exhibits on its western face the Rood beam, at a considerable height above the loft, with a painted rood substituted for the more ancient carved one, the socket of which may be observed on the beam. The tympanum forms a complete barrier from the Rood upwards, but it is pierced with sundry small quatrefoil and other openings, which would have enabled its original occupants to view the sanctuary.

The Ten Commandments, the Creed and the Lord's Prayer would sometimes be painted on the tympanum, as at Pennant Melangell. In 1560 strong recommendation were made for the tympanum to be used for this purpose when the Commissioners noted that people would spare no cost on their private houses, whilst God's House was allowed to fall into disrepair and wall coverings destroyed, thus leaving places of worship desolate of all ornaments. There is a strong suggestion here that the time had come for greater attention to be lavished on the churches.

In 1547 concerted efforts were made to remove the rood and all other images. At Llananno, there were twenty-five images of Old Testament prophets and saints on the screen and they were all removed. The church was rebuilt in 1877, and in 1880 when the screen was replaced, new images were made, which, although new, correspond faithfully to the images of the fifteenth and sixteenth centuries.

As rood lofts were being taken down, many parishes erected new galleries at the western end of their churches for the use of the singers. In 1576, Archbishop Grindal asked the churches:

> Whether your rood be altered, so that the upper parts thereof with the soller or loft be taken down unto the cross-beam and that the said beams have some convenient crest put upon the same?

With the removal of the loft, it was a great temptation for many churches to feel that there was no need for the screen, and if money was not available for maintenance, then they were left to decay until such time as they had to be removed on grounds of safety. However, it is important to note that no instructions were given for screens to be removed – it was the whim of the clergy that was responsible for the destruction of most of them.

Parts of a Screen

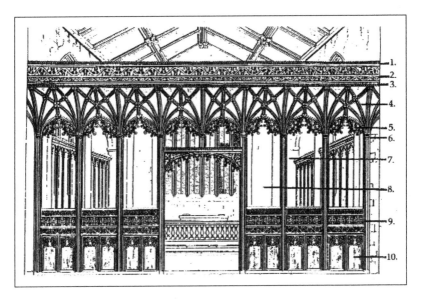

1. Cresting
2. Carved cornice
3. Upper rail
4. Fan vaulting with bosses at the intersections of the ribs
5. Lattice top to the bay
6. Cap to the columns
7. Muting
8. Bay (screen with 8 bays, 2 bays forming the entrance to the chancel
9. Fretwork panel
10. Latticed panels with added ornaments

Chapter 9

Misericords

Screen decoration was not the only opportunity that appealed to the medieval craftsman and excellent examples of his work can be found on bench ends, tabernacle work, and especially so on the misericords.

A misericord is a hinged wooden seat which, when tipped up, presents a corbel-like projection seat for the user to rest upon when in a standing position. They therefore, offered support for monks or canons who were able to rest, without seating, as they stood through interminable divine offices such as Lauds, Prime, Tierece, Sext, Nones, Vespers and Compline. In addition there would be Matins at midnight or shortly afterwards, and High Mass would have been celebrated daily when the whole community would be present. They would also need to celebrate a private Mass. In these daily services, the monks would have had to stand for at least forty-two periods.

The medieval monks would experience considerable discomfort by standing through such a succession of long services. As a concession to the elderly and disabled, they were originally allowed to use crutches and in time the misericord was devised (from the Latin for 'pity' or 'mercy'). It is estimated that about 3,500 misericords still exist in Wales and England. In Wales 132 have been recorded, but some of these are modern. Whilst misericords were usually in choir stalls of cathedrals and former monastic or collegiate churches they are also found in some parish churches. Most of them date from the thirteenth century to the late fifteenth century, and therefore they are the earliest treasures that many churches possess.

Although these seats offered but little opportunity for the craftsmen to demonstrate their skills, they do display remarkable imagination and inventiveness in their execution.

Whilst we may not know the names of those medieval craftsmen, the sightseer who wishes to understand the mentality of ordinary people in the middle ages will find a rich reward in even a superficial study of the carvings on Gothic stalls, particularly those of the misericords. In an age which was lavish in the use of fine craftsmanship it was natural that these corbels, although seldom seen, should be decorated with carvings, and the work gave a rare opportunity for self-expression for the carvers employed. The subjects chosen by the carvers provide information about the middle ages that may not be recorded in any other form. They not only show that the carvers portrayed animals and birds, but more importantly, they give a glimpse of how people lived and their relationship with each other. History books will relate how rich people of every generation live, but the misericords show ordinary people at work and at play. They show fields being ploughed and sown, the killing of animals, the shearing of sheep, and cows being milked. They also show them enjoying their few leisure hours drinking with their friends and also some very aggressive family quarrels. Some of these half-hidden carvings are so finely worked that they immediately make us aware of what we have lost by the almost total destruction of major works of wood sculpture by the iconoclasts.

It would appear that there was no need for the carvers to conform to any logical or, indeed, religious decorations. They were free to give full reign to their imagination. It is surprising that so few misericords convey sacred subjects, and they were not expected to provide any religious instructions to an illiterate congregation. The lack of Biblical subjects and the portrayal of saints in the carvings does provide an insight into the religion of the middle classes of the period, whilst sport, jesters, romance and satire are frequently found. Misericords have been described as 'bawdy and earthy, fantastical and a celebration of legends, folklore, the life and traditions of the common people, a Bible, a Bestiary or a Book of Hours carved in wood'. The opinions and prejudices of the craftsmen on music, art and the preaching of the friars became evident in their work, and immortality in all its forms did not escape their lash. Their work certainly gives us a realistic impression of medieval life.

The influence of religious patrons can be observed in the early misericords, but as the years progress their influences became less important and the craftsmen chose their own subjects, and interesting though they may be, some are very difficult to understand today. Some also reflect local influences and even contemporary political alliances. These craftsmen were clearly capable of executing any form of imagery that their clerical patrons desired, and did not veto the inclusion of some subjects that would be considered unsuitable even by today's standards.

Many of the subjects were chosen from the Bestiary of the Middle Ages that gave descriptions of animals and beasts both real and imaginary. Some of these images were credited with spiritual and miraculous remedies, together with allegorical significance, and people were encouraged to follow the example of some and to reject others. They therefore formed suitable subjects for the carvers.

In an age renowned for its fine craftsmanship, it was only natural that the misericords, although seldom seen, would receive the same careful attention. Any development in their style was limited only by their use, and there was no need to follow any particular arrangement of subjects. They usually consist of a raised motif beneath the corbel and between two subsidiary carvings, known as supports, which are generally different in design and subject matter from the centrepiece. The carver, however, had to ensure that there should be unity between the three motifs, but this was not always achieved. One way to overcome this problem was to carve leaf patterns on the supports, but in Ely cathedral, for example, the carver was able to overcome the problem and ensure unity with all motifs by using Noah's Ark as the main subject: on the left support he carved a raven eating a carcass and on the right side a dove with an olive branch in its beak.

The variety of subjects displayed is quite remarkable and as no subject appears to have been forbidden, it was not unusual for subjects of a sexual nature to be included: some subjects can only be described as pornographic.

The animals depicted would have had a special meaning, as can be seen from the following examples.

Amphisbaena

In Greek mythology this was the symbol of evil and of the devil. This allegorical beast has dragon-like wings and a head on both ends of its body, thus enabling it to move with cunning in either direction. It became to represent a man living two lives. Despite the meanings attributed to it, it is still to be found on a number of screens, as at Llananno and Llanwnog, and on a number of misericords.

Fox

Alexander Pope wrote about the fox in the following words:

> The fox obscene to gaping tombs returns
> And wolves with howling fill the sacred quires.

The fox can be see quite often on misericords and numerous legends have been woven about it. It can sometimes be seen as dressed in a monk's habit and preaching to a congregation of hens. One misericord in St David's Cathedral the fox is dressed in woman's clothing with a headdress fastened with a large pin, and on another, dressed with a cowl. In Gresford church it is seen preaching from a pulpit to a congregation of nine hens and a cockerel.

At first glance, it may appear that such representations are unsuitable adornments for a church, but as the priests often accused the mendicant friars for being lazy and corrupt, they would have welcomed any form of satire on their hypocrisy and lust.

Pelican

One of the Bestiary subject most popular with the medieval carvers was that of the 'Pelican in her Piety' shown standing on the edge of her nest, bringing back to life the fledglings she had killed in a moment of exasperation, with blood from a self-wounded breast. This was considered a most appropriate subject since it symbolized man's redemption, through the blood of Christ, for his sins. An example of the Pelican can also be seen on the Jesse window at Llanrhaeadr as well as on a number of misericords.

Owl
It is not often that animals and birds have been accurately portrayed on the misericords, but the owl is one exception where it is invariably shown correctly. Since the owl is a night bird and does not see very well in the daytime, it is sometimes shown being attacked by a flock of small birds. It was considered an unlucky omen by the Romans but revered by the Greeks for its wisdom. One writer referred to it as 'funeral owl and monster of the night'. Medieval carvers adopted the Roman concept and the owl's nocturnal habit led them to consider the bird as a symbol of the Jews, obstinately preferring the darkness in their own beliefs to the new daylight offered by Christianity.

Elephant
Whilst the elephant may seen an unlikely subject for a misericord, a number of examples have been found, and some show the elephant with a castle on its back. Crusaders returning from the wars in the Holy Land, and other travellers, would tell of enemy warriors going into battle on the backs of elephants protected inside wooden towers or castles, with the castle representing strength. As many of the carvers had not actually seen an elephant, it was sometimes portrayed having the feet of a horse, and sometimes having ears like a dog. It was also taken to symbolize Adam and Eve's innocence. In the Bestiary, it was thought that it only gave birth to one offspring in its life.

Eagle

Large numbers of lecterns are to be found in the form of an eagle with outstretched wings. It has been shown as diving into the sea and emerging with a fish in its claws. To the early Christians, the fish represented Christ, the sea was the world, and the fish represented the Christians Christ saved from the world. An eagle with a fish caught in its claws is to be found on the screen at Conwy. It also represents St John, as it could climb higher towards heaven than any other bird.

Green Man

This is a figure of a man either holding up bundles of flowers as foliage, or a human face peering through a screen of foliage which emerge from its mouth. It is found in a variety of forms on screens, bosses and misericords, and was popular in Europe as well as in Britain. The Green Man is generally regarded as a descendant of pagan tree-worship prevalent in Europe before Christianity turned the groves into sites of Christian worship. The once-sinister subject came to represent the Rogation procession, which brought the blessing of the Church to the spring fields. After the Reformation, the processions gradually ceased to be an ecclesiastical observance in England and now survives only in the walking of parish boundaries on or about Ascension Day, although this practice also has ceased in most parishes.

Lion

In the Middle Ages, the lion was the symbol of strength and dignity, and according to the Bestiary, it breathed upon its cubs, which were born dead, and brought them back to life after three days. The lion, therefore, came to represent the Resurrection and considered a most worthy subject for the misericords. It had also been long used in heraldry and was consequently popular with the carvers.

Griffin

In ancient writings, the Griffin was represented as a creature with four legs, wings and a beak – the front part representing an eagle and the back part a lion. It was said to inhabit areas where gold and precious stones were abundant, and when strangers approached to gather these riches, the creature would leap upon them and tear them to pieces, thus chastising human avarice and greed. The Griffin thus became a suitable subject for misericords and it can also be seen on a number of Welsh screens.

Phoenix

The ancient Egyptians believed that the Phoenix lived for 500 years, and at the expiration of that time it built itself a nest of twigs on which it died by setting the nest on fire and burning itself alive. From the ashes came forth another Phoenix. To Christians it became the symbol of the resurrection and of immortality.

St David's Cathedral

Because of its location, it is not surprising that the sea has influenced the carved woodwork to be found in the cathedral. Two of the misericords reflect this. Shipbuilding was an industry largely ignored by the carvers, but one misericord at St David's shows two shipwrights at work on the hull of a vessel:

one man is using a hammer and caulking the boat, whilst his companion is enjoying a meal and drinking from a shallow bowl, and tools of their trade are also shown. Both men are wearing smocks, caps and boots. The other misericord shows four men rowing a boat and one of them is seasick. According to tradition, this represents St Govan on his journey to Rome to obtain the correct form of the Mass. On the way he nearly died of seasickness, and the carver has chosen this moment for his carving. When Govan recovered, he rebuked his companions and admonished them for over-eating when they should, in fact, have fasted. These two misericords might have been taken from a longer sequence of pictures rather than just two portrayals. The legend preserves the tradition of an unbroken cultural contact between Wales and the continent after the Roman period and the arrival of St Augustine. In a period of which there is so little record, it is of some historical importance. The misericords at St David's are dated between 1493 and 1509 and there are twenty-eight of them in total but seven are modern.

It is clear that the artistic licence given to carvers of the Middle Ages did not pose any real problems to that congregation, but some images were far too risqué for Victorian worshippers, and in the nineteenth century five misericords in Chester Cathedral were removed and destroyed, as they were considered indecent for the staid worshippers of the period.

A study of misericords also leads to a much wider field as they show how comprehensive the visual arts were in medieval churches. Although the building as a whole may not have been accessible to everyone, it nevertheless reflected everything that went on outside its confines. Misericords show that church authorities, and the craftsmen they employed, were neither sentimental nor fastidious. The early church was strong enough to allow caricatures of its clergy, but it was only very seldom that their doctrine was mocked.

But what was really behind the particular art form that is to be found in the misericords? Before the Reformation it was believed that the purpose of art was to mock and satirise. These particular art forms became means for Christian to use against Christian. The monks disliked the friars and despised the parish priest, who in turn despised the monks for the loss of the great tithes and despised the friars because they claimed the fees for marriages and confessions. In reality, however, the carvers satirised preaching rather than religion. Bishops had been trying to persuade the priests to preach to their congregation, and some bishops went so far as to prepare sermons for them to use, but their efforts were not successful. From the thirteenth century it was the friars who satisfied that particular need.

Although the friars travelled the country in their mission, they did establish a number of houses in Wales – for instance, at Brecon, Rhuddlan, Bangor and Denbigh. At Llanfaes in Anglesey the friars were provided with a house by Llywelyn Fawr (Llywelyn the Great). The Grey Friars took an active part in the Owain Glyndŵr uprising and when Owain attacked Cardiff, the Friars' House was almost the only building left standing by him. On the other hand, when Henry IV came to Wales he destroyed the priory at Llanfaes because of their support of Owain's cause.

Crosses were placed by parishes in their cemeteries and on the roadside and it was there that the people gathered to hear the friars preaching. A number of these early crosses are still to be seen in Wales. In the cemetery at Llaneilian, Anglesey, the remains of Eilian's Cross is still standing and there are three steps supporting it on which the friar would stand.

One of the most outstanding crosses in Wales is the huge *Maen Achwyfan* (Stone of Lamentation). It stands by a lonely crossroad north east of Holywell and is nearly 11 feet high. It is exquisitely carved, with an ornate wheel-head cross, and the shaft is covered with intricate interlaced carving. Although nearly 1,000 years old it still represents the tenacity of the Christian faith.

In their turn, the friars themselves became very unpopular because it was considered that they had become too mercenary.

Chapter 10

Llanfaes Priory and Beaumaris Church

Early in the thirteenth century, the Order of St Francis came to Britain, and by the Reformation had established some thirty Houses. The friars' popularity was, in part, attributable to their preference of going out into the world instead of withdrawing from it like the monks. They attracted large crowds by their preaching – a practice which was later to breed increasing resentment and hostility among the clergy and the monasteries.

There would be only a small number of friars in each House and they were committed to the ideals of absolute poverty as set out by St Francis. Although their Houses reflected their poverty, their churches were popular burial places for the rich and noble. To those who had been buried in the Grey Friars cowls, certain important privileges were granted, such as the remission of one-fourth part of their sins. Some knights, and others of rank, would take the friars' habit in their last days and were received as professed brethren of their order. This action was treated with scorn just before and after the Reformation, and examples of their scorn can be found in the misericords. Milton wrote:

> And they who, to be sure of Paradise,
> Dying put on the weeds of Dominic,
> Or in Franciscan think to pass disguised.

The friary at Llanfaes was sited not far from Beaumaris, Anglesey. It was established by Llywelyn ap Iorwerth, Prince of north Wales between 1230 and 1240. It was here that Siwan, the daughter of King John, was buried. In 1414, Henry V gave a Charter to the Friary. It refers to the destruction caused by Owain Glyndŵr, and the fact that regular services were not being held there. The Charter calls for regular services to be resumed, and continues:

> considering that the aforesaid house was the foundation of our ancestors, formerly Kings of England, and exists by our patronages, and also that in the same house the body of the daughter of King John, our ancestor, as also that the son of the King of Denmark and also the bodies of Lord Clifford and of other, lords, knights and esquires, who in the Welsh Wars in the time of our illustrious ancestors, were slain and that remain buried, and we, willing therefore, that divine service in the aforementioned house should be maintained, and there thenceforth continued, we grant for us and our heirs, as far as in us lies, that in the same house there be for ever eight brethren, there to celebrate divine service, and for ever pray to God for our good estate and that of our most dear brethren and others of our blood and descent, and for our souls when we shall have departed this life, and likewise for the souls of our father and mother, and of our ancestors and of those in the aforesaid house, as is before stated buried, and of the faithful deceased, of which eight brethren, indeed, we will that two be of the Welsh nation, with regard to the food of themselves and others, for their abstaining of things needful for their sustenance.
>
> In the testimony whereof witness the King at Westminster, the third day of July, 1414

The Priory remained in existence until dissolved by Henry VIII. Fragments of the stained glass were undoubtedly removed to the church at Beaumaris. The chancel seats of the church could also have come from Penmon.

The church at Beaumaris is also associated with the castle and consequently it was built on an English design. A number of early reports give quite different accounts of the number of seats in the chancel. In 1810, Sir Richard Fenton reported that there were eight seats there. Stephen Glynne reported later that there were twelve seats there and each with a canopy. Today, there are twenty seats but only twelve are original and there are no canopies. There would certainly have been a rood screen and loft but they have long since been removed.

Twelve of the misericords are original, and in the centre of each is carved a half figure of an angel holding a shield. Nothing has been carved on the shield. Various figures are carved on either side of the angel:

(i) Head of a King and Head of a Queen.
(ii) Head of a man with long flowing hair, long moustache and forked beard. Head of a man with moustache and beard with a hood over his head.
(iii) The head of a bishop with mitre and vestment and a clean-shaven face. The tonsured head of a friar.
(iv) The head of a man with curly hair and a clean-shaven face. The head of a woman with her hair trussed on each side and a turbaned head-dress, her gown open in front with a falling collar.

Chapter 11

Symbolism in churches

The cathedrals and early churches had been built for a godly and devout, but largely illiterate, populace. Carvings, symbols, stained glass and wall paintings were used to make the churches more popular and acceptable for the congregation, whilst at the same time, serving as a means of informing them of the church's teaching. Artists and craftsmen had devoted their lives to the work, and the clerics and noblemen vied with each other to provide the best decorations for their churches. Despite all the work done by the despoilers of the past, thankfully much of the beauty can still be seen, and an understanding of the symbols used by the early artisans and artists will only enrich any visit to these early churches and emphasis the importance that was placed upon them.

Whilst the imagery of the early Eastern church had remained important over a long period of time, the Reformation was to bring about a completely new emphasis with the destruction of the icons and imagery which had been so important in the people's lives.

But what do we mean by a symbol? The *Shorter English Dictionary* describes it as 'a thing regarded as typifying or representing something else'. Poets over the centuries have offered their own interpretation. Keats wrote:

> When I behold the night's starr'ed face,
> High clouds, symbols of high romance.

Perhaps William Blake gives the best definition of all:

> To see a World in a Grain of Sand,
> And Heaven in a Wild Flower,
> Hold Infinity in the palm of your hand,
> And Eternity in an hour.

In the words of St Thomas Aquinas (1225?–1274), 'man cannot understand without images. They can only express concepts that language alone cannot express'.

Christian symbols started with beginnings of early Christian communities, and simple symbols used in the first 300 years of Christianity gradually gave way to much more complicated and artistic emblems. Christian art represents the lifetime work of countless outstanding artists and carvers and the Church was their principal patron.

To many who regard churches as museums, the meaning represented by the symbols may very well be lost, but an understanding of their meaning will enrich their visit and may still serve as a teaching aid as they did for their earlier audience. Whilst the cross is the most recognisable symbol of Christianity today, this was not always the case. For the first three centuries it was not used openly as a Christian symbol.

The fish is an ancient Christian symbol and predates the cross. It was a sign used by early Christians. The Greek word for fish is *icthus*, which can be read as an acronym for the Greek phrase *Iesous Christos Theou Huios Soter* (Jesus Christ, Son of God, Saviour). It was used by the early Christians as a secret symbol, so as not to draw attention to themselves at a time when the Church was suffering persecution. It also has a number of inner meanings and has been found in catacombs as well as in Celtic manuscripts, and it was used to signify the human soul swimming through the waters of baptism. The early church also regarded the fish as a symbol of the Eucharist arising from its imagery in the miracle of the Feeding of the Five Thousand.

The Cross

It was only by the passage of time that the cross came to be accepted as the universal symbol for Christians. Originally, the cross and the crucifixion were seen as instruments of capital punishment and widely used in ancient times. Today, it is to be found in every church in the land, and it appeared as the Rood over the chancel screen. It was also removed during the Reformation as a means for the Church to distance itself from the Roman Catholic church. The empty cross now signifies God's power and hope. As a rule, the altar was to be left bare between the ninth and eleventh centuries, but in the thirteenth century, Pope Innocent III decreed that a cross should be placed on the altar at the beginning of Mass. Protestants varied in their practices until the Reformation, when reformers tended to be against any form of ornamentation and altars were swept bare once again. Today, it is the universal practice for a cross to stand on the altar and generally accompanied by at least two candlesticks.

A variety of crosses can be found. In the church of St Isho in Partrishow, Breconshire, there are consecration crosses marking the points where the church was consecrated, and five such crosses have been carved on the two stone altars in front of the screen. These are the only surviving stone altars in Wales. Such crosses may also be found on the walls of some early churches. The ritual of consecration is intended to sanctify the building and dedicate it to God.

1. Latin cross – the most widely used today.
2. Wheel head cross – this form has Celtic association with the head of the cross contained in a circle. The shaft is often filled with a tightly woven web of Celtic interlace and ornaments.
3. Eastern or Russian cross – this has two crossbars with the lower slanting bar near the foot of the cross representing the support for the feet.
4. Anchor cross – This represented the message of hope and was a symbol used before the Christian period – both sure and steadfast.

Sacred Monograms

A Monogram consist of two or three letters interwoven to form a symbol. Sacred monograms composed of initial letters and abbreviations of Greek and Latin words have been used from the early days of Christian art. Outstanding examples are to be found in Irish and Northumberland manuscripts. One of the earliest and best form of the monogram is the LABARUM, being a simple combination of P placed over X, the Chi and the Rho, the first two letters of the Greek word meaning Christ. Another popular monogram is the three letters IHS being the first three letters of the Greek word for Jesus. Other letters used, but not in the form of a monogram, are INRI being the first letters of *Iesus Nazarenus Rex Iudaeorum* – (Jesus Christ King of the Jews). The first and last letters of the Greek Alphabet ALPHA and OMEGA are also used – representing Christ as the beginning and the end.

Labarum   I.H.S.   I.N.R.I.   Alpha and
                                                   Omega

Numbers

Numbers were also important features in the ancient churches,
particularly the number seven, which was considered a holy
number, as in the seven sacraments (baptism, confirmation,
Mass, penance, extreme unction, ordination and matrimony);
and the seven deadly sins (pride, wrath, envy, lust, gluttony,
avarice and sloth). Trinity windows are to be found, and the
Jews had their Star of David or Star of the Creator, with its six
points representing the six days that God took to create the
world. The Triquetra is an ancient symbol where the three
equal arcs represent the Trinity and its continuous form
represent eternity. Octagonal baptismal fonts are to be found,
with the number eight representing resurrection and new life.

Trinity Window   David's star/   Triquetra   Octagonal
                   Creator's star   font

Animals and Plants

During the Middle Ages everything had a religious or spiritual meaning. The Phoenix, a mythological bird rising from the flames, represented the Resurrection. The Pelican, feeding its chicks with its own blood, was a symbol of the sacrifice on the Cross and the Holy Communion. The Lily was the symbol of purity and its white flowers recalled the Virgin Mary. Occasionally, Christ is seen crucified not on a Cross but on a Lily. One of the symbols most often seen carved on the screens is the vine, which is based on Christ's words 'I am the true vine'. As mentioned earlier, one of the earliest symbols of Christianity was the fish.

Symbols of the Passion

The shield was a popular device in the Middle Ages and often symbols of the Passion would be found on them. These symbols are also to be found on doors, bench-end, screens and on roof trusses. A number of these symbols are to be found on the screen at Llanrwst, Denbighshire. The following are the most frequently found: (i) the cross with the cloth draped over it that was used to lower the body of Christ after his crucifixion – the letters INRI are sometimes carved upon the cross; (ii) the lantern of Gethsemane; (iii) the cockerel of Peter's denial and (iv) the hammer and pincers.

Symbolism in church plans

Traditionally, the congregation in churches face the east and, therefore, are facing the dawn. The nave (from the Latin *navis* for ship) was symbolic of the journey to heaven, a door on the north side was always associated with the devil. Placing the baptismal font near the door signifies that only through baptism could a person be accepted into the church. Covers were fitted over fonts, and were sometimes locked so that the holy water could not be taken for superstitious purposes. To approach the altar it was necessary to go under the cross (or rood) that was placed on the screen, again signifying that only through the cross, and all that it represented, could salvation be found.

Saints and their symbols

Saints also had their own personal symbols which again can be found on the screens. St Peter has the keys of heaven; St Paul, a sword; St James, a scallop shell and a pilgrim's staff (a number of churches, to this day, use a scallop shell for baptisms); St Mark has a winged lion and St John has an eagle.

Chapter 12

The churches of St Mary and St David, Newtown

The churches of Montgomeryshire have enjoyed a richness of carved woodwork over the centuries. It has been estimated that nearly 300 screens have been recorded at some time or another in Wales, and thirty of those were to be found in Montgomeryshire. With almost the uncontrolled destruction that occurred after 1540, it is very fortunate that so many of these treasures remain.

In 1909, the Report of the Royal Commission on Ancient and Historical Monuments in Montgomeryshire reported that:

> The parish churches of the county have, without a single exception, been more or less restored, some several times, within the last half century. In too many cases the restoration consisted of the total demolition of the earlier edifice . . . and the erection of a new church, sometimes on a different site as at Llandysil. In the greater number of cases the new building is placed on old foundations, but the architectural features have given way to others that were deemed of better taste. Almost every church must have possessed a fine oak screen of which that of Llanwnog is the best surviving example.

As the work of reconstruction and destruction took place, the contents of the churches also suffered. For example, in 1836 the medieval screen at Llangurig was taken down and offered for sale, as firewood, for any one who had an interest in it. Today, parts of that particular screen grace a country house near Welshpool.

In 1856, the screen that was originally at St Mary's church, Newtown, was transferred to the new church – St David's – but large sections of it are now lost. The screen at St Mary's was considered the finest in Wales, but the surviving sections of it, together with the detailed drawings and notes of the Revd John Parker, which he made between 1829 and 1836, give an indication of the loss, when these are compared with the screens at Llananno and Llanwnog.

The history of the screen at Newtown is a perfect example of what happened throughout Wales, but what is really surprising is the fact that so much of the screen has remained.

The old church of St Mary's at Newtown was in need of urgent repairs in the beginning of the nineteenth century. A few yards north of the church flowed the Severn. It frequently overflowed its banks, and as the floor of the church was about a foot lower than the churchyard, the river used to flood into the church. The rectory nearby was also frequently flooded.

By 1811, the condition of the church was so bad that it was decided to build a new church and rectory. The new rectory was completed by 1813, but thirty years were to elapse before a new church was built. In the meantime, the old church deteriorated year by year.

The reason for this delay was the objection raised by the Revd G. A. Evans of Newtown Hall. Although he was not the priest of Newtown, he did have certain rights in the old church, and he was most anxious to retain those rights. He was entitled to eight seats (with spaces for eight persons in each seat), together with the right to seat forty persons in the gallery.

These objections were eventually resolved by the Court in 1843, when it ruled that Mr Evans was not entitled to keep his privileges, and the way was now clear for the construction work on the new church to begin. It was completed by 1847.

Despite this, one big problem remained. What was going to happen to the ancient screen? There were reports in the press which disturbed some churchgoers and historians, as the intention was to sell it.

The old church had a solid tower on the west side and a wooden bell tower on top of it – a design which is characteristic of a number of the churches found in the Marches. It had a chancel and two aisles, and the body of the church was whitewashed; there were eight pointed wooden arches separating the chancel from the aisle. In the past the wardens would obscure the wooden beamed roof except for the southern chancel, where three fairly large angels were carved.

The main glory of the church was the ancient screen. In 1810 the traveller Richard Fenton, who was on a journey through Wales, described it like this: 'The Rood-loft as to carving, gilding and painting is perhaps the most perfect thing of its kind in the kingdom, said to have been brought from Abbey Cwm-hir. There are no two compartments alike'.

Fenton, like many of his contemporaries, connected this screen with Abbey Cwm-hir, but Canon Maurice H. Ridgeway, an expert on Welsh screens, says that this is of parish creation. He dates it from the end of the fifteenth or beginning of the sixteenth century.

The most detailed reports of this screen are to be found in the manuscripts of the Reverend John Parker who, between 1827 and 1844, was rector of Llanmerewig, which is not far from Newtown. He made a detailed study between 1829 and 1832, providing accurate measurements for every aspect of the screen, as well as several pictures of its various parts. During the years in which he studied the screen Parker saw a significant decline in its condition, and although he never drew a picture of the entire screen, his descriptions and his fine illustrations enable us today to admire the work of the early craftsmen and to realise how great our loss is that so many of these treasures have been destroyed.

On Parker's first visit in 1829 he said that the condition of the screen was so bad that he could not imagine how it had originally looked – this was after the visit by Richard Fenton in 1810 which contradicted this, claiming that its condition was almost perfect. He measured the screen and found that it was twenty-two feet wide and stretched across the two aisles. In one manuscript he says:

> In other chancel screens we have specimens of rich carving and the practice of ancient carpentry that may be discovered in all its interesting details, but here in addition to all this, we have a specimen of ancient colouring, by which the rules may be discovered for this rare branch of Gothic art. The skilful contrasting of blue and red, of purple and gold, upon a dark brown ground are here displayed. The methods of preserving the spirit and effect of carving, when gilt and coloured, are to be observed here, and the general effect which this colouring produced was, I think, dreamy, shadowy brightness combined with most elaborate workmanship.

It is obvious that much of the damage was done to the screen before John Parker saw it in 1829, but his reports enable us to create a fairly accurate picture of how it was originally. This screen was not only the glory of the church but also of all of Wales. There is no doubt that this was the finest in the country.

Despite the harm which had already been done to the screen, a decision was made in 1856 to pull it down once again and use parts of it to surround the three walls of the chancel in the new church. To achieve this, 10 feet had to be cut off and the screen's height lowered. In 1875 the chancel was re-built and the screen was pulled down once more; it lay in the rectory cellar for some years. After saving it in 1909, it was used to panel the chancel afresh but a large part of it remained in the rectory.

In 1938 what was left was used to surround the Chapel of the Virgin Mary, but new posts had to be made for it as the original ones had broken some years before.

Although a variety of the original colours were to be seen on the screen in 1829, the authorities had to burn them off in 1875 and hide them with varnish, so that today only a few colours are visible here and there.

Although it is a blessing that so much of the screen remains, there are many lessons to be learnt for the future by studying its history. We cannot afford to lose treasures like this.

Chapter 13

Chancel screens II

Llanengan, Caernarfonshire

The Church of Saint Engan, or Saint Einion the King, stands about a mile and a half from Abersoch on the Llŷn Peninsula. In the Middle Ages this church was a popular destination for pilgrims on their way to Bardsey Island. There were close connections between the church and the Abbey on Bardsey. The greater part of the church dates from the end of the fifteenth century and the start of the sixteenth. The tower was added in 1534 and the date is to be seen on it. There are two aisles to the church, and the arcade that splits the two is very similar to that which is seen in Llangwnnadl church and also in Bangor Cathedral.

There are two screens to be found in this church – the north screen which separates the body of the church from the chancel, and the south screen which is in a similar position on the other side of the arcade. Only above the south screen is there a rood loft. These screens share the same tale – they both came from the old Bardsey abbey, but they are of parish manufacture and design. The form of the south screen is similar to the one in Llanegryn church in the county of Meirionnydd.

The two screens which are in this church are totally different to each other; by looking at them it is obvious that much damage has occurred to them over the years, and the fact that the patterns on them do not always follow naturally shows that new pieces have been set into them in years gone by, and that some pieces have been set incorrectly.

On the west side of the rood loft there are thirteen plain panels without any decoration at all. Were there paintings of the saints on them at one time? The east side is far more decorated, with eleven panels of carved fretwork. On these too there are a variety of interesting symbols such as a pierced heart surrounded by a crown of thorns, and hands and feet which are pierced, a wreathed snake which is a symbol of eternity, and also the staff of life. The friezes on both screens are notable for the variety of carvings to be seen, as well as for the ingenuity and sensitivity of their workmanship.

On the eastern side of the north screen a grotesque image can be seen of the head of a man sticking his long tongue out – very similar to the Green Man, but this one does not have leaves coming out of his mouth. As well as this, there are small carvings of a man holding a book which has the picture of a woman praying on it.

Clynnog, Caernarfonshire

The church of Saint Beuno in Clynnog, Caernarfonshire, was a popular destination for pilgrims on their way to Bardsey Island. The church was founded in 630 by Beuno, and an ecclesiastical college was set up there – *y clas* (cloister) – which was an establishment unique to the Celtic church.

On the south side of the church there is Saint Beuno's Chapel, which is connected to the church tower by a narrow entrance called '*Y Rheinws*' (the lock-up), as the place was used at one time to hold the troublemakers of the area. It was in Beuno's Chapel that the respected poet, hymn-writer and schoolmaster Ebenezer Thomas (1801–1863, bardic name

Eben Fardd) maintained his school.

In the book *A Description of Caernarvonshire (1809–1811)*, Edmund Hyde Hall mentions that 'The roof is of open woodwork but that of the chancel is ceiled with wood and painted in imitation of clouds, among which are seen the dove and various figures of angels. The execution is sufficiently mean.'

Not far from the church is Beuno's Well and in the olden days it was believed that its water could cure the sick.

Over the centuries many changes have affected the church, as one would expect, but the screen which dates from the sixteenth century is still in place. The Canon Maurice Ridgeway argues that this is not a screen in the Welsh tradition, but one of English design. It's a simple screen, and all the fine carvings that are characteristic of the Welsh screens are not to be seen.

When John Leland visited the church in 1536–39, he said that the building had been restored a few years earlier. In 1505 the church was consecrated by Archbishop Skevington, Bishop of Bangor, and although he only visited the episcopy sporadically between 1505 and his death in 1533 he undertook a number of improvements in his cathedral.

Shortly after finishing the work in Bangor cathedral significant improvements were made to Clynnog church and, as the work is so similar to that done in the cathedral, there is room to believe that the same craftsmen were also responsible for the work on the screen. Unfortunately, no woodwork from the time of Skevington has survived in the cathedral and so comparisons cannot be made.

In 1829 the Revd John Parker visited the church and made

a drawing of the original screen. In 1856 considerable alterations were made to the screen, when the upper parts were removed and replaced with a new section. (See the drawing made in 1829 and the photograph of the screen as it was repaired in 1856 and remains to this day.)

Nant Peris, Caernarfonshire

The churches of mountainous areas such as Dolwyddelan and Penmachno have their own characteristics; this is also true of the churches seen on the Llŷn Peninsula. They all suit their environments perfectly and nestle low against the strong winds. However, the church at Nant Peris, Caernarfonshire, does not fit totally amongst the traditional designs – there is no aisle in the body of the church nor a door on the west side, but there is a transept that was built during the fifteenth century. The chancel was extended during the sixteenth century.

Originally, the screen stood to the west of the transept but it was moved from there and a gallery built in its place. Around 1850 more changes were made to the church; the screen was pulled down and repositioned at the south of the entrance, allowing a small vestry to be created behind it, doing away with the gallery.

This is a very simple screen, but well-suited to the church, as it was in the sixteenth century. It is characteristic of the screens that were erected in small churches in areas such as Snowdonia.

As it has been moved about many times over the years, it is obvious that the screen has been damaged terribly. It has three bays around a central door and on each bay there is a simple fretwork panel. Specialists cannot agree on how much of this fretwork is original, but on close examination it is obvious that it does not all date from the same period. In 1829 there was fretwork above the entrance but it has disappeared by now, and some of the original fretwork has also been damaged. The wainscot panels are very plain, and they have no decoration on them at all. On top of the cornice there was a space for putting candles.

The coloured glass which was set into the screen when the vestry was formed is totally irrelevant and detracts from its original simplicity. In fact, it is difficult to appreciate the fretwork now.

The register of the church which dates from 1776 states that there is a box in the screen to receive money for the poor – Cyff Peris (*Peris' Trunk*) – and this can still be seen today. As in many other churches there is a well associated with it, and the money that was thrown into the well by visitors was used to pay part of the parish clerk's salary. The water from the well is still used today for baptism.

Although the Nant Peris church screen is very simple, it is important as it represents the type of screen that was to be seen in an area like this.

Llaneilian, Amlwch, Anglesey

The majority of north Wales' medieval rural churches were built for the local communities, as they were at that time. Local materials were used and local builders were responsible for their construction, and that is why they are of such great interest to us today. It was eighteenth-century apathy which made the huge task of restoration and rebuilding necessary, and as a result these churches lost their primitive identity.

Unfortunately, Anglesey churches have suffered more than

almost any other county, and in the nineteenth century more than half the churches had been rebuilt, demolished or improved substantially. What we see, therefore, are churches alien to their community and landscape.

Considering all the rebuilding that was necessary, it is not a surprise that much of the medieval woodwork has been lost. Today only one screen remains amongst all the county's churches and for this reason the Llaneilian church screen, near Amlwch, is very important.

This is an oak screen which dates from the sixteenth century. There is much evidence of restoration and all trace of colour has been erased. On the eaves under the rood loft there is an image of a skeleton and above his head there are the words: *Colyn angau yw Pechod* (the sting of death is sin). This is a most primitive image, and its purpose was to educate the illiterate congregation. It is likely that there would have been other images on the original screen, but they have all been deleted. At one time an image of the patron saint had been put on the screen, but by now it can be seen above the vestry door.

The rood loft has open panels with twenty-two moulded pillars. The special characteristics of the screen are the high doors of Perpendicular Gothic design which shut off the chancel from the body of the church; this is a rare example of this design in Wales.

There are two borders of the same size above the screen, and on the lower one the two vine leaves and bunches of grapes have also been carved – which look more like pineapples. The higher border has been carved with trefoil leaves, but from each one part of the leaf has been cut off.

It is unfortunate that so much of this screen has been

destroyed over the centuries.

The pictures of it which date from the 1920s show it to be in much better condition at that time than it is today, but it does have some very interesting features.

Llanegryn, Meirionnydd

The nineteenth century saw a number of churches from the Middle Ages either being left to decay or having their character changed so much that they were nothing like the original buildings. These churches no longer suited their areas, and 'urban' churches with pointed towers were built in their place. However in Llanegryn, Meirionnydd, the original Welsh design was retained when the church was being restored in 1876. The thanks for its escape from the hands of the Victorian church refurbishers should go to W. W. E. Wynne, Peniarth, who was a noted antiquarian in his day and a columnist for *Y Cymmrodorion*. It was he who directed the work of restoring the church. The relationship between the gentry and the churches has not always been a successful one, but in Llanegryn it has been very beneficial.

The first report of the church is to be found in the Norwich *Taxatio* in 1253 when Cymer abbey near Dolgellau received its tithe. The church was consecrated to Saint Egryn before the Cistercians arrived in Cymer, and after this it became known as Saint Mary's Church, according to their usual practice. Since the departure of the monks it has been known to the present day as the church of Saint Mary and Saint Egryn.

Because of the close connection between the church and Cymer abbey it was only natural for some to think that the screen had come from the abbey after its resolution in 1537.

Certainly, there are some who still believe that the monks had carried the screen to Llanegryn during the night over the mountains.

It must be remembered, however, that Cymer was a poor abbey, and it suffered terribly during the wars of Edward I in 1276–77 and again in 1282–83. By 1388 there were only five monks there, and by the fifteenth century their financial resources and influence had declined. In 1535 its income was only a little over £53 a year, and then in 1537 the abbey was dissolved. It would have been impossible under such circumstances for the abbey to give the screen to Llanegryn church. They did not have enough money to finish building the abbey. As well as this, the Lay Brothers – the conversi – had left the abbey a hundred years before its dissolution.

Certainly, the true glory of this little church is the screen and the wonderful rood loft that can be seen there. This again is one of the treasures of the Church. The west parapet has been divided into thirteen panels and there are linear recesses between the panels; in these places small effigies would have been placed. Careful work has been carried out in the past to repair the screen.

The parapet at the eastern side of the rood loft has been divided into seventeen panels and every panel has been carved differently. There are circular, oval and diamond-shaped geometric patterns on them, with leaves and fruit occasionally worked in. The variety to be found in these carvings is incredible and always ingenious, and it is difficult to imagine seeing better panels than these anywhere. The old Welsh craftsmen were very fond of using water lily leaves, and this is seen at its best in this screen.

Llanrwst, Conwy

One of the wonders of the Conwy Valley is the screen in Llanrwst church, Denbighshire. The patron saint of the church is Crwst, a saint who lived during the sixth century. The site of the present church, on the banks of the river Conwy, was chosen by Rhun ap Nefydd Hardd in the eleventh century as atonement for his father's crime – the murder of Owain Glyndŵr's son.

The church was destroyed during the Owain Glyndŵr rebellion, and it was destroyed completely in 1468 by the soldiers of the Earl of Pembroke, but it was rebuilt in 1470.

According to John Parker's reports the screen was in a very bad condition when he visited the church in August 1829, and some parts of it were loose and likely to fall off while other parts had obviously been lost. The clerk did not know what had happened to them. However, Parker found parts of it 'in a heap of dust under the floor of the Reading Desk, two small pieces, one was the front of the larger canopies, and the other was one of the smaller ones'. That image in the words of John Parker speaks volumes about the attitude at the time towards the treasures of the church.

Today the screen is a decoration for the church and very interesting, but it is a screen of English design, although it has to be admitted that there are some Welsh characteristics that belong to it, such as the fretwork which fills the twelve arches. In some features it is similar to the English screen in Clynnog church, Caernarfonshire. The Archdeacon D. R. Thomas says in his volume History of the Diocese of St Asaph that this was a screen from Maenan abbey and that the conversi made it around 1470; however, they had left the abbey 100 years before

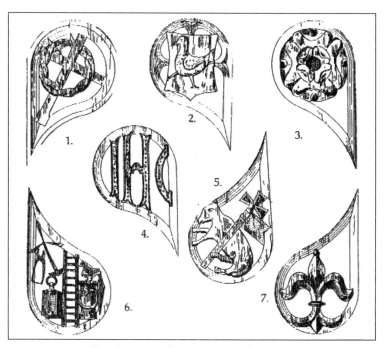

Carvings on the screen at Llanegryn

1. *Cross and Crown of Thorns*
2. *Dove – which is often found on a font and which represents the Holy Spirit*
3. *A Rose – emblem of both sides in the Wars of the Roses, but which is also a symbol of Christ*
4. *IHC – which comes from the Greek word IHCOYC, for Jesus. It is sometimes used instead of IHS*
5. *The Lamb and the Banner – the Agnus Dei (Lamb of God) with the banner of victory. John said, after Jesus Christ's baptism, 'Behold the Lamb of God, which takes away the sins of the world' (John's Gospel, chapter 1, verse 29)*
6. *The Suffering – the hammer and the anvil, the lamp which was carried in the garden of Gethsemane, the ladder; the cock which crowed when Christ was betrayed by Peter*
7. *The fleur-de-lis – symbol of the purity of the lily, because it is a white flower that is connected with the Virgin Mary. It is often shown in the conventional form of the fleur-de-lis*

that. In its form and manufacture, this is a parish screen, and the Cistercians would not have any screen similar to it.

There are a number of interesting carvings to be seen on this screen: for example, symbols of the Passion, a pomegranate, the Lamb and Standard, a cross and crown of thorns. Two borders can be seen on the beams which are under the rood loft and which have been skilfully carved. The lower border includes oak leaves weaving around each other, and the highest includes vine leaves and fruit of the vine interwoven. There is one other border of leaves and fruit above the panels.

The rood loft is still to be seen; it would still have been used by the musicians and singers until the end of the nineteenth century. There are twenty fairly plain panels with small recesses and crockets in them to hold effigies or candles originally. Thomas Dinley said in 1684 that he had seen a carved effigy of Christ that was once, he said, above the screen, but it is likely that he was referring to the 'Christ from Mostyn'. This can be seen today in Bangor Cathedral, and it is possible that it was never part of this screen.

Llanwnnog, Montgomeryshire

Llanwnnog is a small village in Montgomeryshire with a cluster of houses and an ancient church. At the end of the sixth century Saint Gwynog founded his church here. The present church dates from 1862, but it is on the same site as the original and shelters the close community who live in its shadow. It's a simple church in design, but with a tower that is completely characteristic of the churches of Montgomeryshire and Radnorshire.

Around the church are several imposing yew trees and in its

graveyard can be found the grave of John Ceiriog Hughes displaying the famous *englyn*:

> Carodd eiriau cerddorol – carodd feirdd
> Carodd fyw'n naturiol;
> Carodd gerdd yn angerddol,
> Dyma ei lwch – a dim lol.

> *[He loved musical words – he loved poets*
> *He loved living naturally;*
> *He loved music with passion,*
> *This is his dust – and no nonsense.]*

There is no architectural characteristic separating the body of the church from the chancel apart from the screen and the rood loft. The screen is a good example of the work of the craftsmen of Montgomeryshire, and although it does not exhibit the same perfection as the screen in Newtown before it was damaged, or the woodwork which is still seen in Llananno, it still remains a very notable screen, and has drawn attention throughout the centuries since it was constructed at the end of the fifteenth century or the beginning of the sixteenth. There are several reports of it in the years between 1825 and 1915, with a number of them mentioning its worsening condition from one year to the next through carelessness or lack of understanding and sympathy when restoring it.

The screen and the rood loft are independent of each other and the screen does not support the rood loft as it would normally; there are five narrow bays on each side of the entrance to the chancel. On the northern side fretwork panels are to be seen, but the panels that were on the southern side have been lost. The cove cornice under the loft creates a ceiling of ingenious and complicated work. There are two long panels on the western side of the screen beautifully carved with vine leaves weaving around each other. Another panel can be seen with oak leaves and branches and acorns interweaving with each other. The work and the patterns are completely characteristic of the work that is seen on Welsh screens.

A number of bosses can still be seen on the screen today, although some of them have been lost and others used on the church ceiling. On them are the symbols IHS and M. The letter M is to be seen exactly above the entrance to the chancel, and this conveys to Catholics the idea that through the Virgin Mary one enters heaven. On this side, too, were a number of small recesses which held portraits of saints at one time, but they were destroyed during the nineteenth century, possibly because they reminded the congregation of the papism of days gone by.

The rood beam has been carved with leaves and pomegranate fruits like the screen at Newtown, which again suggests local manufacture.

Llananno, Montgomeryshire
The church of Llananno is in Powys on the main A483 road from Newtown to Llandrindod Wells, some three miles to the south of Llanbadarn Fynydd. There is no village there, as such, and the church can be seen in a field about 300 yards from the main road and on the banks of the river Ithon.

There is no information available about the original church apart from the fact that its patron saint is the Celtic Saint Anno, c.780. It's possible that the church has been on the site since the arrival of the Normans. Llananno is a small parish, about four miles by three, and today there are less than forty inhabitants in it.

In 1871 the old church had to be demolished, and the building which is seen today was built on the same site. The ancient screen was pulled down and in 1880 the church was rebuilt again. In design the church is characteristic of rural Welsh churches and fits naturally into its landscape.

Although the church does not draw attention from the outside, there is a magnificent screen to be seen within. With the loss of the screen at Newtown the Llananno screen can lay claim to being the most highly decorated in Wales. Once again we are indebted to the work of the Reverend John Parker for his detailed descriptions and at least twenty-four drawings of the screen. He made several visits to the church whilst making his study, and it is sad to discover how the state of the screen deteriorated from year to year until 1841. On his first visit in 1828 his description of the church was 'the docile and unsightly barn, for the church at Llananno has no pretensions of any sort of architectural beauty'.

Parker had great expectations for the screen when he went there in September 1828, but by reading his report it can be seen that he was somewhat disappointed. Parts of the screen had been torn away and almost the whole screen was seen to be distorted. As well as this, the majority of the crockets on the canopy, as well as one whole border, and nearly half the panelled ceiling were missing. Despite this, there was enough of the screen left for him to wonder at the work of the craftsmen who were, in his opinion, able to create this kind of ebullient luxury. Although parts of the screen were to be found here and there around the church, he said, 'I succeeded in restoring some original patterns of panelling which were all broken in pieces, altho' they merited a better fate'. He spent two whole days studying the screen, at the same time admitting that he had much more work to do before he could fully appreciate it. However, Parker realised at once that this screen was one of the best in Wales after the one at Newtown was lost.

By the time of his visit in August 1841 there had been some attempt to renovate the screen.

When the screen was put back in 1880 a number of changes had to be made as the new church was a little wider than the one that was there before, and so there are five bays on each side of the entrance to the chancel instead of the four that were there originally. What is surprising is that no one took advantage of the opportunity to remove it completely in 1880, the reason being the old superstitious beliefs that were still held at the time.

In the days of John Parker there were twenty-five small recesses on the front of the screen, and in these would have been the statues of the Apostles and the Old Testament prophets and so on, but they were all destroyed at the beginning of the Protestant Reformation. Despite this, new figures were put in the recesses in 1880, and although they are modern figures, they suit the screen. The figures represent Noah carrying the Ark, Abraham, Joseph, Aaron, Moses, Samuel, David, Solomon, Elijah, Isaiah, Jeremiah, Ezekiel, Jesus Christ, Peter, Andrew, James, John, Philip, James the Lesser, Thomas Bartholomew, Mathew Simon, Judas and Matthias. Under the figures there are two long borders of leaves and fruit and on the lower border the Amphisbaena with the branches of the vine coming out of its mouth. The vine leaves, water lily leaves and the pomegranate were very obvious symbols in Greek mythology, with the first two representing life and the last death, and these three symbols were carved on a number of Welsh screens from the start of the sixteenth century.

After refuting the idea that this screen had come from Abbey Cwm-hir, some argued that it had been made in either Hereford or Leicester. Despite this, its construction shows clearly that it is a Welsh parish screen, and the carvings are different to those that are seen on screens in England. One must remember of course that there are examples of screens of totally Welsh manufacture to be seen in England such as St. Margaret's, Hereford and Daresbury, Cheshire.

Llananno's screen shows clearly the imagination and vitality of Welsh craftsmen at their best. The wonderful colours which were characteristic of the work from the Montgomeryshire centre have been removed, but we can only be amazed and thankful for the outstanding work which is displayed on this screen.

Partrishow, Breconshire
Partrishow church stands some five miles from Crickhowell on the slopes of the Black Mountain in Breconshire, and in this isolation the population would never have been numerous. The full name of the church is Merthyr Issui (Ishaw or Isho) in Patricio. The fact that the church is in such a remote place has been the means of saving it from the problems of the centuries. The road that leads up to it crosses the river Grwyne Fawr over Pont yr Esgob (*the Bridge of the Bishop*) which is, according to tradition, named after the time when Gerallt Gymro was preaching in the area with Archbishop Baldwin.

A stone's throw from the church is Ffynnon Isho (*Isho's Well*) where the saint had his cell, and the place also where he was martyred. In the wall at the back of the well there were small recesses where pilgrims would put sacred effigies or relics.

There are a number of interesting treasures in the church. Inside can be seen a Saxon baptismal font and on it the words '*Menhir me fecit i tempore Genillin*' (Menhir made me in the time of Cynhillyn). Cynhillyn was the Lord of Ystradwy before the Conquest. The Book of Llandaf states that Herwald, Bishop of Llandaf from 1055–1103, consecrated Merthyr Issui church in memory of the martyr, Patrico. This dates the font therefore between 1055 and 1066.

Without any doubt, the main treasure of the church is the rood screen and loft which can be seen in it, which date from the end of the fifteenth century. It is obvious that the site of the church was too remote for the early travellers to come across it and so there are very few descriptions of it. However, in the month of May 1804 Richard Fenton was there and in 'Patrico where I saw the most perfect and elegant Rood Loft now standing in the Kingdom, of seemingly Irish Oak which fortunately has escaped either white-washing or painting' and in this, the Partrishow rood loft is unique. It is viewed today as it was left by the craftsmen at the end of the fifteenth century.

Unfortunately the screen itself has deteriorated terribly and a lot of the fretwork in the divisions, as well as the plain unadorned panels of its wainscot, have been broken.

The beam which is under the rood loft is sumptuously carved. Three borders can be seen on it, with each one wider than the other as it rises. On the lowest border there is a line of deeply carved flowers, and on the middle border there is a version of water lilies but without the expertise which can be seen in the Llananno screen. Each part of the pattern has been made of six leaves and three small flowers. On each side of the upper border there is a dragon with an open mouth, sharp teeth and a long, twisty tail. From his mouth come vine branches with two leaves with bunches of grapes between them. The ridge that is seen above the three borders is of fairly new work.

However glorious the work to be seen in the three borders, the main glory of this loft is seen in the work on the parapet. This is divided into seventeen fine fretwork panels, which are so elaborate that they resemble lacework. Every panel measures 8½ inches in width and is 25 inches high.

On the beam above the parapet there are eighteen holes cut to hold candles.

In front of the screen are two stone altars and on both five crosses have been cut. This is the only example of altars of this kind in Wales which are still in their original position.

On the west wall in the body of the church there is an image of death holding a sickle in his right hand and an hourglass and a spade in his hand and over his left arm. There is also an old trunk here carved from a single piece of wood which is very similar to the trunk seen in Clynnog church, Caernarvonshire.

If this small church was not on the travellers' paths then it is clear that it was not on the spoilers' paths either, and as with some other examples in Wales, its location has saved it and its treasures so that we may enjoy them today.

Chapter 14

Epilogue

No study of churches can avoid mentioning the importance of the repair and renovation works which have taken place. The work of repairing churches from the Middle Ages, together with all the carved woodwork which is within them, has drawn much attention over the years and has very often been criticised harshly. There are several examples in Wales where the churches and their contents have been totally ruined by those who were 'restoring' them.

The architect Gilbert Scott was very strongly critical of those who destroyed the work of this early period, although he in turn was criticised fairly strongly for the same transgression – for example, there is no original woodwork remaining in Bangor Cathedral.

Whatever we think about the Victorian restorations, one must remember that a number of churches in that era were in very bad condition, and for us today they would look sorrowfully plain and bare. The furniture in them belonged to a number of periods and was irrelevant to the requirements of the church at that time; there were a number of box pews to be seen piled against each other, and a pulpit of two or three levels in a number of small churches. As a result of the call for renovation, the Victorian architects were only too willing to demolish the box pews and take down the big pulpit, along with the boards that showed the Ten Commandments and so on, and accept once more the Gothic style.

Although the Victorians were criticised for what they did to the churches, we must also express our appreciation of them. It was they who were responsible for the installation of a large number of glorious, stained glass windows in many a church, as well as the production of exceptional decorative ironwork.

It must be remembered that the work done during the age of Victoria was completed in a period of less than seventy years, and in that time the architects and craftsmen had to learn anew many of the Gothic styles which had almost been forgotten. Our churches contain a great deal of the best work of the period and yet there is no doubt that heritage is not of the greatest importance to our own generation today.

However, our churches are not intended to be museums. They are intended to be an important part of our towns and of our parishes. If churches are closing today, and the congregations diminishing, reports still show that an increasing number of people like to visit them and enjoy and wonder at the treasures that are such an important part of them.

One must question what is going to happen in the future. Are we, at the beginning of the twenty-first century, ready to shoulder the burden of sustaining and preserving the churches, so that we may pass them on safely to the next generation?

When we enter the occasional ancient church in the countryside and admire the rood screen and loft which date from the Middle Ages, what could this wood have to say to us? It has been witnesses to huge changes over the centuries and has seen many changes in the act of public worship. It has seen human deeds at their best and at their worst.

Touching this wood today, and feeling the marks of the early craftsmen, we bridge a gap of over 500 years. What will it have to say about us in the future, I wonder? The responsibility weighs heavily upon us.

Bibliography

M. D. Anderson, *The Mediaeval Carver* (Cambridge University Press, 1935)

M. D. Anderson, *Misericords* (Penguin Books, 1954)

W. Ambrose Bebb, *Machlud y Mynachlogydd* (Gwasg Aberystwyth, 1937)

Archaeologicia Cambrensis (magazine)

Revd William Bingley, *North Wales, including its Scenery and Antiquities and Customs* (2 vols) (London, 1804)

Francis Bond, *Woodcarvings in English Churches – 1. Misericords* (Oxford University Press, 1910)

Francis Bond, *Screens and Galleries in English Churches* (Oxford University Press, 1908)

F. Bligh Bond and D. Camm, *Roodscreens and Roodlofts* (2 vols) (Isaac Pitman, London, 1909)

J. S. Curl, *Victorian Churches* (B. T. Batsford, London, 1995)

Stephen Friar, *The Companion to English Parish Churches* (Chancellor Press, 2000)

W. A. Griffiths, *Tales of Welsh History and Romance* (1915)

Hughes and North, *The Old Churches of Snowdonia* (Jarvis and Foster, Bangor, 1924)

J. W. James, *A Church History of Wales* (A. H. Stockwell Ltd, 1945)

Dr Johnson, *Diary of a Journey into North Wales in 1774* (London, 1816)

Francis Jones, *The Holy Wells of Wales* (University of Wales Press, 1992)

Francis Kilvert, *Diary January 1870 to March 1879* (3 vols) (Jonathan Cape, 1961)

Samuel Lewis, *Topographical Dictionary of England* (1833)

Sir Samuel Rush Meyrick, *The History and Antiquities of the County of Cardigan* (1809)

E. J. Newell, *A History of the Welsh Church* (Elliot Stock, London, 1895)

H. L. North, *The Old Churches of Arllechwedd* (Jarvis and Foster, Bangor, 1906)

J. H. Parker, *Introduction to Gothic Architecture* (London, 1891)

Edgar W. Parry, *Y Teithwyr yng Nghymru, 1750–1850* (Gwasg Carreg Gwalch, 1995)

Edgar W. Parry, *John Parker's Tour through Wales and its Churches* (Gwasg Carreg Gwalch, 1998)

Thomas Pennant, *A Tour of Wales* (2 vols) (London, 1784)

Augustus Welsby Pugin, *An Apology for the Revival of Christian Architecture in England* (London, 1843)

G. L. Remnant, *A Catalogue of Misericords in Great Britain* (1969)

Robert Richards, *Cymru'r Oesau Canol* (Hughes a'i Fab, 1933)

Canon Maurice H. Ridgway, article in *Archaeologica Cambrensis* (1943) and others

Robert Roberts, *A Wandering Scholar: the Life and Opinions of Robert Roberts* (University of Wales Press, 1991)

Sir Gilbert Scott, *Personal and Professional Recollections* (1870)

Archdeacon D. R. Thomas, *History of the Diocese of St Asaph* (3 vols) (1906–1913)

Walter Walsh, *The Secret History of the Oxford Movement* (London, 1899)

F. E. Warren, *Liturgy and Ritual of the Celtic Church* (Oxford, 1881)

Sir John Wynn, *The History of the Gwydir Family* (London, 1770)

Yr Haul (magazine)